WHAT OTHERS ARE SAYING ABOUT BEYOND THE EDGE OF THE WATER

If you didn't think discipleship was a lost, art you will now. It's harder than ever to help teenagers want to follow Jesus let alone do it well. Steve's insights from personal experience and good research breathe fire into the soul of every disciple maker and gives hope by providing a way forward tangible for everyone. This is as good as cultural exegesis gets!

Dan Boal, director, Alliance Youth

Bold and timely, Steve shares fresh inspiration, compelling vision and practical action steps every leader can take to disciple their students to truly change the cultural landscape of our world.

Hannah Gronowski, author, speaker, founder, and CEO of Generation Distinct

For the most important mission in the history of mankind, Jesus chose to invest His time, effort, and heart in discipling a band of new believers. But *how* did He do it? How are we doing it in today's complex culture of competing worldviews? Where the goalposts of morality keep moving, even within the church; where many consider the highest moral virtue to be the affirmation of every belief and behavior; and where perceived Christian values are dismissed as unloving, unenlightened, and irrelevant. In this book, drawn from Scriptural example and his own experience, Steven tackles the question of what it takes to guide young Christians into a life of biblical discipleship. May his hope and optimism in the rising generation, combined with his insights and strategies, inspire you to also invest your time, effort and heart in making disciples who love the Lord their God with all their heart, mind, soul, and strength.

> Dr. Wess Stafford, president emeritus, Compassion International, Author of *Too Small to Ignore: Why Children Are the Next Big Thing,* and *Just a Minute: In the Heart of a Child, One Moment Can Last Forever*

In a world full of fear, anxiety, and doubt, Steven delivers a way to help young people experience Jesus, surround themselves with community, and live out authentic faith.

> Jonathan McKee, author of more than 20 books including *Teen's Guide to Face-to-Face Connections in a Screen-to-Screen World*

If you are hoping to connect with students, understand culture, and guide students into a biblical model of discipleship, here is a helpful resource for you. My friend Steve has a particular knack for explaining complex ideas, cultural influences, and youth culture in practical, easy to understand ways. This is a wonderful book for anyone concerned with reaching and equipping the next generation.

> Sean McDowell, PhD., associate professor, Talbot School of Theology, Biola University, speaker and author.

Engaging the head, heart, and hands of youth is vitally important for creating disciples. This book is one of the few that really addresses all three aspects and treats them with equal importance to the discipleship process. Youth pastors and parents should take note. We cannot create Christ followers without explaining how the Gospel is relevant to every aspect of their life.

> Hillary Morgan Ferrer, co-author and general editor, *Mama Bear Apologetics: Empowering Your Kids to Challenge Cultural Lies*

BEYOND THE EDGE OF THE WATER

STEVEN M KOZAK

BEYOND THE EDGE OF THE WATER

RECLAIMING BIBLICAL DISCIPLESHIP FOR A RISING GENERATION

P.O. Box 544
Winona Lake, IN 46590
bmhbooks.com
800-348-2756

Beyond the Edge of the Water
Reclaiming Biblical Discipleship for the Rising Generation

Copyright © 2020 by Steven M. Kozak

ISBN 978-0-88469-363-5 (print)
        978-0-88469-364-2 (ebook)

REL109030   RELIGION / Christian Ministry / Youth

Published by BMH Books
Box 544
Winona Lake, Ind.
bmhbooks.com

DEDICATION

To my tribe:
Your love and tolerance
are a gift from God.
Thank you.

CONTENTS

Introduction

RECLAIMING BIBLICAL DISCIPLESHIP

I am the Way, the Truth, and the Life.

Jesus (John 14:6)

I really like Jesus, but I have no intention of following him.

I was shocked, but that's what several of my high school students told me. They sincerely believed that to be a Christian only meant they had to like or appreciate Jesus and *some* of the things He said. To them, Jesus was nothing more than a model citizen. Loving like Jesus meant accepting people for who they were and affirming them in whatever lifestyle they chose. To do otherwise was a heinous act of hatred. This is the kind of thinking behind an ideology called Moralistic Therapeutic Deism. Essentially, it's the belief that there may be a higher power looking down from above, but it is not directly involved in human affairs. The key concerns are happiness and being a good person. And being a good person means setting aside disagreement and any sort of objective truth. Truth now presupposes exclusivity. And exclusivity is hateful and hurtful. This is precisely why it's easier to ignore Jesus as the only way, the truth, and the life—the only means by which we can get to the Father (John 14:6)—and confine Him to a space that fits our culture's demands.

A New Standard for Truth

In more than a decade of teaching, leading, and discipling students, I learned this kind of thinking is not at all an isolated or a rare occurrence. In fact, it's normal. Maybe disturbingly normal. So typical, it has become embedded into the culture of the rising generation. Perhaps even indoctrinated. Sure, a lot of people—students, adults, and everyone in between—like Jesus. He's got that chill vibe, a Gandhi sort of swagger. Jesus sure seems like the great example of love and acceptance. But follow Him? Be a Christian? That notion, the notion of discipleship—the kind of discipleship we get straight from the pages of Scripture—has been lost in the busyness and noise of our relativistic western culture.

The root cause is our culture's recent dive into what is now called post-truth. By now, it's likely you have heard the term. After all, it made front page news in 2016 as Oxford Dictionary's word of the year. The term denotes the "circumstances in which objective facts are less influential in shaping public opinion than appeals to emotion and personal belief." The term fundamentally places feeling over facts and experience and perception of reality rather than reality itself. So if Descartes described truth as *"I think, therefore I am,"* a post-truth advocate would argue, *"I believe, therefore I am right, because that's how I feel."* In other words, the validity of truth is always subject to feelings.

Even Jesus is subject to this same new standard. How you view Him, which instructions you decide to obey, and how you interpret His actions are entirely based on one person's experience and feelings. Unless you were born after the mid-1980s—the beginnings of the Millennial generation—the shunning of objective truth and rational thinking might seem entirely ridiculous. But for everyone younger, it is accepted as truth. From college to elementary school, students are being taught that all ideologies are equal, given equal time and attention, and all ought to be embraced simultaneously. Since experience guides truth, everyone's truth has equal validity. I know what you're thinking: *This can't be true because it can't work.* And you're right. In terms of worldviews, two opposing ideologies cannot both be true at the same time. You can't believe Jesus to be the only way to the Father but also believe in reincarnation. They don't fit, yet here we are. And by the looks of our current cultural climate, it's here to stay.

The Challenges Ahead

What my students were expressing is indicative of what researchers have now determined: the western world is officially post-Christian—actively rejecting Christianity and the message of the gospel. My students—and many others like them—have no tolerance for a Jesus who demands exclusive obedience, objective morality, denial of self, and absolute truth. While many people would still consider themselves spiritual in some sense, and perhaps even possess faith in a higher power of sorts, there is a mass exodus from the idea of organized Christianity. According to the latest research from both the Barna Group and Pew, nearly half of Americans note their religious identity as "none." That number jumps to more than 50 percent in Europe. This means that people are far less likely to accept any one religious system as true and another as false. This is forcing churches to face some new challenges.

Nowhere is this challenge more important in Christendom than in our youth groups and families. Parents and youth leaders work tirelessly to ensure that our students are discipled and given every opportunity to own their faith so that they might walk in faith boldly as they enter adulthood. But here is the problem: *culture is winning.* It is the world that has captivated the attention of students. It is actors and musicians like Alec Baldwin, Brad Pitt, Taylor Swift, Drake, and Post Malone who are the priests and prophets of the modern age, taking full advantage of their platform to push their own version of the "good news." And it's the new digital reality working around the clock to define our students' identity. Today's youth are faced with challenges we never saw coming or could have predicted, and our efforts to meet these challenges are falling far short. Our ability to make disciples is fading fast. At every corner, it seems culture is setting a new standard and creating deeper division between the world and the church. The church steeple rising over our communities that once served as a beacon of hope for the world is now seen as a disease that needs to be eradicated.

Perhaps I'm being too harsh. Perhaps I'm just being an alarmist. To be honest, sometimes I think I might be. But whether it's entertainment becoming more sexualized, the growing influence of the LGBTQ community, drag queens reading stories to children at the public libraries, or the suppression of Judeo-Christian values in the broader culture—that is, the deeper we walk into a post-Christian reality, the greater the need for Christians to be engaged and impacting culture. So what's the answer? What are churches and families supposed to do?

There may have been a time when churches and families could simply ignore culture—stick to teaching students the Bible and sound morals. Surely even the most wayward children would make their way back, right? After all, twenty or thirty years ago, the Bible still stood as our nation's moral compass, there was still a universal understanding of sin, and much of the social justice around the world had its roots in the gospel. But times have changed, and I believe there is a cultural tidal wave with the church standing in its path. We tried to keep the water out, but when we weren't looking, it began to seep through the cracks. In our efforts to fill buildings in hopes people will hear the gospel, and in our efforts to connect with a fast-changing culture—with every other organization outpacing the church in its ability to connect—we are showing signs of compromise. Let me give you three quick examples.

Example 1: The Church is ignoring the Bible.

In his book, *Hope of Nations*, John S. Dickerson commented that "Any ministry or family that abandons the authority of Scripture is one generation away from abandoning Christianity entirely." It is no surprise when we hear atheists, agnostics, or other opposing worldviews discount the Bible's authority over our lives. However, twenty years ago, that opinion was still considered the minority. This is no longer the case.

In our post-truth, post-Christian culture, the western world has gone so far as to demand the removal, influence, and relevancy

4

of Scripture. To do otherwise is to actively promote a hate-filled agenda—creating a perceived need for the church to compromise. In our pursuit to appease culture, to be relevant, liked, retweeted, and shared, the church is dangerously flirting with putting her needs over God's desires. Our sermons have gone from exegetical to motivational, treating the Bible as a series of suggestions rather than authoritative truth.

Now I know this is not true of every church in every place, but in our highly distracted age, it is far too easy to reduce discipleship and spiritual formation to nothing more than weekly church attendance and perhaps the occasional small group meeting; forgetting that we hold the very breath of God in our hands. I have seen first-hand Bible teachers marginalize Scripture in an attempt to connect students to God; picking and choosing what to teach so we don't offend. However, our understanding of morality, our foundation of truth, and the purpose and mission of humanity are laid out in Scripture. It is divine. It is inspired. And it is infallible. To attempt the Christian life without it is like playing football without a football.

Example 2: Our service has become more social than it is gospel.

There is no shortage of philanthropy, non-profits, organizations that donate earnings, even individuals who live incredibly generous lives. Their stories inspire us to be like them. Giving is contagious. There may not be a shortage of giving, but there is a shortage of the gospel. I know several Jesus-loving Christians who have created non-profit organizations looking to provide medical care, clean water, food, and even build entire communities—all of which are important, necessary, and noble tasks. Yet in many of these, the gospel is mysteriously absent, expecting that if we love enough, love will automatically translate into a gospel message. It is almost as if we are disguising Jesus into a more palatable version the world can stomach.

But our world's poverty will never find its solution in our attempts to remedy external needs. The answer is not external, it is internal. Jesus and the gospel are not peripheral benefits of our service to others or some kind of unintended advantage. The solution is the gospel. The answer is Jesus. The mission of every follower of Christ is not only to serve as a reflection of the risen Christ bringing redemption and rescue to ends of the earth, but also to proclaim the gospel and the reason for the hope that lies within.

Generally speaking, our students appreciate the ability to give back. They feel the need and are more than willing to lend a hand. But the good they are eager to do falls far short of good without the gospel.

Example 3: Sin is a constant moving target.

We desperately want to believe in the goodness of humanity. In fact, our children are taught as early as elementary school that people are inherently good, and we want nothing more than to hold on to that sense of delusional hope. The result is an increasing need to excuse many of the world's sins. If people are generally good and we are not to judge another's understanding of truth, then we have no basis for calling certain behaviors sin.

The line between what is moral and immoral is a continually moving target. The times when we sought after biblical, family values are becoming a distant memory. We have replaced the doctrine of total depravity with a new doctrine of acceptance and affirmation of nearly any kind of behavior. After all, who are we to judge? The result: no need for Jesus' atoning sacrifice, or resurrection, or even Jesus at all. If sin is marginalized, then what do we need saving from?

The New Digital Reality

On some level, I imagine these trends (and many others like them) have always had some kind of influence on culture, the church, and specifically, our students. But things are changing much faster and with greater force than what previous generations have experienced. And we have the new digital reality to thank.

Social media has created a world where students are living alternative lives. I don't mean fake profiles or obscure handles that mysteriously omit ages and genders. I mean legitimate Snapchat, TikTok, and Instagram accounts, where students can present themselves in any way they choose or in any way they are pressured to. Our students' social media presence is as if they are on stage for the entire world to see. And to judge.

In the world of social media, reality is whatever students create it to be. It's a space where everyone looks great, every vacation is an epic adventure, and every gathering is the best night ever. But social media also has a way of catching us at our worst moments and logging them in the chronicles of digital history for eternity. For many, it's like trying to cross an ocean with no idea how to swim. With that comes real pressure. For most adults, when we were teenagers, the social forces could be all but forgotten in the quiet tranquility of a bedroom. I remember being able to escape that kind of stress and anxiety when I was a student. Today there is no escape. The influence of culture is in every bedroom, in every family vacation, in every success, and every failure. It seems that privacy is a thing of the past.

Discipling our students requires us to be keenly aware of the digital self that lies behind that student who sits every week in the third row, second seat on the left, the student in the front row who has all the answers, or the quiet kid in the back row you see once a month. There is a more in-depth story to our students than most of us ever imagine possible, but the story is told in places some of us never venture to.

So What if We Are Getting Discipleship Wrong?

The rising generation is not the future of the church—they are the church. The kid you are raising, coaching, or mentoring is already making an impact in his or her community. Yes, our investment in them today prepares them for a future that has deep-seated implications for the church in the days ahead. But maybe, more importantly, our investment today has an immediate impact both in terms of the church right now and the surrounding culture. If you lead youth in any way, you are shaping the church right now for right now.

We putter along thinking that the methods we use are adequate when our results are just short of terrifying. Students continue to abandon the church in droves, and the generations to come are being raised never having stepped foot inside a church. But we continue to believe that if it worked for us as students, then it must work for students today. We work hard hoping for a payoff we may never see. At the same time, we ignore what is right in front of our faces. There will always be students who graduate, leaving us wondering if their faith will survive college and beyond. Some of them pull through, and some don't. But we can't ignore the strength and power of our students' faith in the present. We can't ignore the growing number of students who have never read a Bible, never attended youth group, and don't have Christian parents. And we can't ignore the fact that the greatest means we have of reaching and discipling the next generation is the next generation.

Stop Just Hoping

As a teacher, I had the privilege of standing on stage during the commencement ceremonies for our graduating seniors. My role was to read their life verse as they made their way across the stage diploma in hand, smiling ear-to-ear, filled with a penultimate sense of accomplishment. Next up: college.

But were they going to make it? Were they ready? Would their faith withstand the cultural onslaught that was coming straight for them like an out-of-control freight train? With every hug or handshake came an overwhelming wave of anxiety. Would I ever be sure of my influence? Perhaps not definitively, but indeed, there were some steps I could have taken to at least allow myself to sleep a little better at night.

Our school's entire infrastructure of discipleship was geared toward loading students up with knowledge, skills, and a few experiences in hopes it would be enough to carry them through college. We basically viewed college as a barren desert. No food or water for the next four years. Our task was to supply them with enough to make it to the fertile lands of family and career. We called it preparing them for the future.

But it wasn't. What we called preparation completely ignored discipleship. What we hoped would set students up for future success did nothing for their current experiences. We gave students everything we counted on them needing, sprinkled some magic fairy dust on it, and hoped it would somehow translate into a disciple of Jesus on mission for the gospel. We hoped for disciples instead of making them.

Stop Just Equipping

I don't believe this scenario is limited to the graduation stage of my little Christian school world. I think the same is true for the church. It is nothing malicious or ill-intended. We are still focused on discipleship. Well, maybe not quite. More specifically, we are focused on equipping God's people, hoping that it makes disciples. But there is more to discipleship than just equipping. It is more than a distribution of tools for any job that may come their way. I can purchase every tool available at Home Depot for my students and they will still have no clue how to use them to build a house. The same is true of discipleship. Giving our students all the tools they need means very little if we never demonstrate how to use them and then give them ample opportunity to master them.

Long before college served as the appropriate next step for youth to gain the skills necessary for life and career, the more common method was an apprenticeship. As far back as ancient Egypt, Babylon, and even Israel, young men were taught a craft by working alongside a master craftsman. A practice that even expanded to medicine and law. Working alongside a skilled master

9

craftsman allowed for teaching, coaching, correcting, and mentorship. Every moment was a teachable moment. The same could even be said of young Jewish boys selected to follow a rabbi. To become a disciple was to become an apprentice. Colleges and universities equip students by giving them every conceivable tool needed for the journey ahead. An apprentice is taught along the way, how to become a master of those tools. Walking with those we mentor in their journey, teaching them and guiding them in each step, and providing the means to master the tools we provide is the blueprint for disciples who make disciples, and fulfilling the Great Commission (Matt. 28:16–20).

I believe it is time to reconsider our methods for raising up and discipling a new generation. It is time to truly meet our students' needs with the power of the gospel. It is time we reclaim biblical discipleship. It's time we stop compromising, trying to please others in hopes they will show up to church. I believe it's time we show our students what it truly means to follow Jesus, what it means to sacrifice, what it means to commit, what it means to live a new resurrected life in Christ, what it means to live on mission, and what it means to love. God has invited us into a new experience of who He is and the life He has created for us. It is time we get beyond church attendance, devotionals, and small group meetings as our standard means of making disciples and enter into the journey He calls us to embrace. The journey is wrought with commitment and sacrifice and overflowing with a new kind of love, a new kind of community, and a new kind of self.

It is time we invite our students into this journey. But where do we start? Easy. We begin this journey by stepping off the sand and into the river.

1
TRUST WHAT IS ON
THE OTHER SIDE

Trust wholly in Christ; rely altogether on His sufferings; beware of seeking to be justified in any other way than by His righteousness. Faith in our Lord Jesus Christ is sufficient for salvation.

John Wycliffe

The cool morning air pressed against the general's face as he made his way about the camp. Israel was setting out from Shittim to set up camp on the banks of the Jordan River. After three days, Joshua gave his officers the green light to prepare to cross the river (Joshua 3:1–2). For as long as I can remember, this has been a favorite passage of mine. I often wonder what that moment would have been like, for Joshua, his officers, and the rest of the nation of Israel. What would the mood, the atmosphere, or maybe the tension have been like? A long journey neared its end. The goal was waiting across one river. What was on the other side? What would it all mean?

For more than forty years, the nation of Israel wandered the desert, learning what it meant to be a people belonging to the Creator of the world. The intention was that Moses, the man who led them out of Egypt would be the same man who led this great nation-to-be into the Promised Land. But he wouldn't see the dream become a reality. The fear and disobedience of the people delayed the realization of the promise until a new leader rose up and the time was right. Joshua would be the one to take charge and lead the people into a new reality, a new kingdom, and a new life.

The nation of Israel camped on the eastern border of the Jordan River about twenty miles south of a town called Adam and just north of the Dead Sea, the final resting place of the Jordan. I imagine the mood of the camp was thick with anticipation, eager to get on with it. Perhaps many of them had that feeling in the pit of their stomachs, one part nervous, one part excited. On the one hand, nervous because of the unknown on the opposite bank of the river. On the other hand, excited because the stories of a promise made to Abraham, the promise of Israel becoming a great nation, were finally coming true.

The instructions were simple. Wait for God. Don't over analyze, chart the best path, or wait for the right moment. Joshua tells the people to consecrate themselves—be holy, clean, and tapped into the divine because "the Lord will do amazing things among you" (Joshua 3:5).

The people gathered their things and prepared to witness the unimaginable. At certain times of the year, the river is only a small trickle of water, but in the spring, when the snow in the mountains melts and flows downstream, the river rises so high it begins to overflow the banks. As the priests made their way toward the water, they were not approaching a trickle of water or even an ankle-deep stream. They were about to step into the Jordan River at peak flood stage with the current rushing past. The river has the potential to be so treacherous that its depth and current would take a person off their feet and send them on a deadly path into the Dead Sea. Approaching the Jordan River to go stand in it, at its deepest level of the year, its most dangerous time of the year, makes absolutely no sense. Eager to see the Promised Land, anxious to see God move within His people, and longing to take part in the divine mission, the priests led the way.

As their toes touched the edge of the overflowing waters of the Jordan, a miraculous thing occurred: the rushing water stopped flowing almost twenty miles upstream. The remaining water emptied into the Dead Sea, leaving a bed of dry ground to travel over.

There stood the priests of God, holding the ark of the covenant, the very presence of God on dry land in the middle of the Jordan's path. The more than two million people of Israel made their way across, because their God, a God of deliverance and rescue, the God who brought this nation out of Egypt, the God who made a band of slave people into His nation, the God who made a promise and made good on that promise, made Himself known. What seemed unthinkable became a new reality—an invitation into a new kind of kingdom.

Discovering Discipleship in the River

Crossing the river was more than just another miracle moment or the next really cool thing God did among His people. Crossing the river wasn't a means to an end; it was a new beginning. Experiencing this miracle was about letting God go ahead, trusting Him in the moment for what would happen next. The Promised Land wasn't just a destination; it would be how God would reveal Himself to the rest of the world through Israel.

In fact, I believe this entire moment of Israel crossing the Jordan River into the Promised Land is indicative of what it means to be a disciple. Whether we are just stepping into the water or learning what it means to live on the other side in a foreign nation, God is demanding we take that next step. Believing in Jesus means following Him across the river. Discipleship demands following Jesus into what seems to be the impossible. It requires perseverance in the face of what seems to be sheer stupidity.

And before we ever attempt to help our students take the first step, we need to consider for ourselves if we are willing to cross and enter a land utterly foreign in every way? Are we ready to join God in His mission regardless of the cost? Are our students prepared to do the same? This is the stuff of discipleship that few talk about. Because just crossing the river isn't going to be enough. Like the Promised Land, the other side is not the end of the journey—that is not where discipleship ends. We have to live out the life of a disciple in a foreign land.

So maybe you're thrilled that God has brought you to this point—the edge of the riverbank, but perhaps the shoreline is far enough. A comfortable lounge chair, some suntan lotion, and a lifetime relaxing, waving to the passersby as you admire *their* great boldness and faith. Maybe you really do want to cross, but you need more information. You Googled some data on the river, checked out the seasonal information, you have familiarized yourself with the flood-stage patterns, and you are looking for the best place and time to cross. You know that some women and children need to cross, so you make plans to get them across first, design and implement strategies to construct rafts to carry supplies and personal belongings. Of course, you will cross. When you're ready.

Maybe fear is getting the best of you. Maybe you're standing on the bank of the river, and no matter how hard you try, you cannot move. The sheer impossibility has your mind spinning out of control. You can't fathom why anyone would think crossing this river is possible, let alone surviving on the other side. That fear eventually leads to doubt—even unbelief. You begin to rationalize, staying safely on dry land. Rather than doubt that God will actually show up, you don't bother giving into the chance. Or worse, you feel that sense of fear and doubt because you think you have no business crossing that river. You have no business enjoying the other side. *Who am I?* you begin to ask. *What could God possibly do with someone like me? I am undeserving, unbelieving. I am a traitor and a hater. I am not holy enough, righteous enough, loving enough. I am not fit to do the things that God wants me to do.*

If you're already there—on the other side—meaning, on fire and on mission for the kingdom, that's amazing. Keep at it. We need you. But the unfortunate reality for so many of us (and our students) is that before we ever take a step in the mighty river, before we even begin to see what is on the other side, and before we ever get to see the deep, profound reality of who God is and what it looks like to live a life of faith, we will have come up with every excuse in the book. And we will have missed it.

The message to the nation of Israel crossing the Jordan was clear. The Israelites were the people of God, and without Him, they stood no chance. God commanded the priests to carry the ark ahead of the people so they would know that the living God had gone before them, and that He would be with them. But the people had to take a step of faith. As they stood looking out over the water, behind them was captivity, the memory of their slavery, and wandering in the wilderness. Behind them was a kingdom of this world built by their blood and sweat. In front of them was hope, forgiveness, a new nation. In front of them was something that God was building.

Jesus and the Jordan

Fast forward to the first century. Israel had suffered through defeat, exile, and continued captivity from foreign nations. But God was not done doing new things. God was not done moving in history and making Himself known.

> *People went out to him from Jerusalem and all Judea and the whole region of the Jordan. Confessing their sins, they were baptized by him in the Jordan River.* (Matthew 3:5–6)

A thousand years before John the Baptist was baptizing people in the Jordan, the nation of Israel crossed and conquered the Promised Land. They were preparing for what it took to become a nation and to carry out the mission of God. All with God as their king. Now the command was to enter the river again, in obedience, preparing for an even greater conquest, one that would defeat evil and death and establish the kingdom of heaven here on earth. This was not some ritualistic baptism, but a total commitment in preparation for the coming king. And if that is not significant enough for you, Jesus insisted on being baptized as well. But instead of trumpets blaring, the waters parting, and a nation bent on conquest, we simply have Jesus coming out of the water. And with quiet subtlety, the new kingdom had begun. A thousand years before, Joshua told the people to consecrate themselves because God was about to do something. The command was for Israel to prepare herself for a new age and a new kingdom. John's call to baptism was the same call for preparation. "Repent, for the kingdom of heaven is at hand."

Just as God delivered on His promise to the nation of Israel, a much greater promise was unfolding. God showed Israel, on the banks of the Jordan, that success comes through humility, meekness, and obedience. God taught Israel that the only way to the kingdom, the Promised Land, was by following Him. Jesus delivers a greater promise, a greater kingdom, and a greater calling. The coming of the Messiah ushered in a new kind of life and a new kind of kingdom. God promised deliverance from the ultimate exile, the slavery of sin that has entangled the earth since the beginning. However, God had to go before us and do the thing we could not do. Jesus' crucifixion and resurrection gave us the means to enter the ultimate Promised Land and live the life He desires for us.

Just like the nation of Israel, Jesus is asking us to follow Him through the river and to the other side—to bring light into a foreign nation. Jesus is asking us to follow Him to the cross, to do the unthinkable. Jesus is calling us to take on the impossible and make it possible—living the life He has called each of us into—the life of a disciple.

Starting the Journey

Maybe you really desire to follow. You're doing the Christian thing. Your reading your Bible, praying, coming to church, and serving. Life is good. You have a great job and a great family. In quiet times of prayer, maybe you are sensing that God is asking something more of you. Perhaps it's a move; perhaps it's your finances; perhaps it's reaching out to someone. But doing so might disrupt your comfort. Whatever it is. It's a call for trust.

Maybe you have been praying for weeks, or even months, about how God is going to use you. You're standing on the shore, toes dipped in the water, and yet you stand paralyzed. Maybe you have tried and been burned before. Perhaps you have been told by more than one person that what you think God is telling you is impossible. Perhaps you're so unsure of your abilities, and you're listening so intently to what the world is saying, you can't hear the voice of God. So you stand on the shore paralyzed.

Maybe you know exactly what God is asking of you. But you know how crazy it sounds at this point in life. Perhaps you don't have enough money. Perhaps you're just waiting for the right season in life, and then you'll get to it. You want to cross the river, but the timing is not right, the place is not right, and you're waiting on the necessary resources.

Finally, maybe you're not sure you even want to cross the river. What if God doesn't show up? What if He doesn't even exist? What if I get it wrong? You think that there is no way God would ever let you cross into His kingdom and use you, that the calling is not meant for you.

Regardless of where we stand on the bank of the river, God is calling each of us to something greater. He is demanding our trust. Our doubt, our fear, our complacency, and our paralysis are entirely valid if we are crossing under our own power, and by our own resources. But because Jesus went before us, because Jesus fought the battle we could not fight and won the victory we could not win, we can move forward in the will of God with confidence, conviction, and victory.

When you move forward into the mission that God has called you to, all the doubt, the complacency, the fear, the boredom, the self-reliance, the storms, the reluctance, the failure, the safety, the self-righteousness, the guilt, and the apathy are erased. The doubt is replaced with confidence, complacency with movement, fear becomes undaunted persistence, boredom becomes eagerness, the storms are welcomed, and the reluctance turns to readiness. All the failure, guilt, and apathy become passion, forgiveness, and victory.

It is not by our own strength that we cross the river, but by Christ in us. It is not by our own plan and provision that we enter the kingdom, but by Christ in us. It is not by our own power that we carry out the mission, but by Christ in us.

God is inviting us to a life far greater than anything we can conceive or conjure up. He is inviting us into a life in the Promised Land. He has invited us into the life of discipleship. To get there, we must cross. But to cross, we must trust. We must trust that the victory is already determined because He went first. Jesus went to the cross first. We have to become nothing. We must put aside our plans, our preparations, our goals, and our dreams for the sake of His kingdom. Only then, can we be the people that we were designed to be and do the things we were called to do. And only when we humble ourselves can we see Him as something greater.

That is what this book is about. It is about discipleship. It's not about your best life right now or ten simple steps to follow Jesus. Nor is this book a theological dissertation packed with fancy and complex theological constructs. This book is designed to give you and your students simple truth about what it means to follow Jesus across the river and into a foreign land. It will take you back to the Scriptures and to the mystery of who God is and the life He calls us to. It doesn't always follow conventional wisdom. In fact, it's mostly counter-cultural. There is often intense fear, persecution, frustration, and even doubt.

Let's be honest. Sometimes following Jesus looks downright ridiculous. The Israelites sure did crossing the Jordan. But if our discipleship experience is not reflective of the Bible, if it is not a little scary, beyond our own capacity, then it's not discipleship. My goal is to show you what this looks like. I hope to help you and the students in your life understand what Jesus means by taking up our cross, what it means to live totally committed, to die to ourselves. But I also want you to see the life that He desires for you—a life on mission, loving your neighbors, utterly dependent upon the Spirit of God.

It's time we get beyond the edge of the water and step into the unknown. It's a journey worth taking.

2

DISCOVERING WHAT YOU LOVE MOST

Commitment is what transforms a promise into reality.
It is the words that speak boldly of your intentions.
And the actions which speak louder than the words.

Abraham Lincoln

My wife and I sat in the middle of the empty living room. Speechless, frustrated, and afraid, we just cried. Our first kid was due in a few months. We weren't homeless, but we were pretty darn close. It was an income property that had gone terribly wrong; a crashing housing market and renters who neither paid nor took care of the property left it in almost unlivable conditions.

I desperately wanted to tell my wife—pregnant and all—that everything was going to be okay. But let's be real for a second. We were in ministry. We had given our lives, sacrificed a bigger paycheck, and we had a kid on the way! What in the world was God thinking? I would be lying if I said I didn't yell at God for a week straight. I would be lying if I said that I just trusted God and kept moved forward. Instead, I sincerely questioned the whole ministry thing. If this Jesus life would be this hard, maybe it was time to rethink it.

But this moment had little to do with hardship. I knew difficulty would happen—after all, that's life. It was about commitment. In that moment and in many more moments to follow, my commitment to Jesus waned. But not my commitment to my wife or my daughter to come. Why? Simple: when I accepted Jesus, it was not about commitment. In fact, my decision to get married was much more thought through, calculated, and prepared for than my decision to follow Jesus.

For months I agonized over when and how to propose. After my soon-to-be fiancée said yes, we spent nearly a year in pre-marital counseling; and then finally at the altar, we verbally committed to each other for better or for worse. Each step of the way, we were continually reminded that marriage would not be all sunshine, rainbows, and unicorns all the time. Getting married was a moment. Being married is a process. Yet my understanding of discipleship was all sunshine, rainbows, and unicorns. It was only a moment. There was no counseling, no vows—really no commitment. It would never be needed, or so I thought.

Isn't that precisely what we teach our students?

Do No Harm

It stems from a parenting philosophy that aims to protect children—carefully wrapping our kids in bubble wrap, packing peanuts, and clearly marking the package "fragile." It comes from a noble place of wanting the absolute best for our kids. We want every success for them. We want them to experience every victory, only the positive with no pain or evil. After all, what good-intending parent, youth leader, or pastor would wish for anything less? You may remember, a few years ago, the trend of parents watching every move their kids would make ensuring they were protected at all times—we called these parents *helicopter parents*. It was the best means of protecting our children from any conceivable harm, but now we have *lawnmower parents*, who have taken it to an entirely new level. Rather than just hovering over their children, lawnmower parents clear the path of any potential obstacles standing in the way of their child's success.

No matter the good intentions behind it, this trend is setting our students up for failure. We end up preparing the road for our children rather than preparing our children for the road ahead. As a result, we are raising a generation obsessed with safety. Take a glance at any of the latest research being done on the rising generation. It reveals an overwhelming desire to avoid risk. College campuses feature safe spaces at every corner, not just protecting them from real physical threats of some kind, but from the danger of ideas that students might not agree with. On many college campuses across the country, to disagree is to commit an act of violence. Growing up, I wanted to get to college and have a voice so that I could be considered and treated like an adult. Today, students expect the same activism but to be treated as children.

Simply put, the rising generation is in no hurry to enter adulthood. And they aren't ready for it either. There is even a word for it now—adulting. If we are not careful, clearing away the obstacles in the path of our students will damage their faith. It will impair their ability to persevere and hinder their ability to grow in Christ.

I believe our faith depends on it.

Wouldn't it be great if we could promise and deliver a hassle-free, stress-free, failure-free life for our kids and the students we lead? But the reality is that we are never guaranteed that Jesus will take on the role of the lawnmower parent and remove every obstacle and hindrance in our paths so that we might only know peace, prosperity, and unrelenting success. We are, however, promised difficulty, strife, and the filth of sin staining our lives—precisely the reason we need Jesus. Students need the tools and preparation for the journey ahead as it is, not how we would like it to be. Which is precisely how Jesus intended discipleship to be. And it begins with finding commitment.

Finding Commitment

To get a handle on what this commitment looks like, I want to introduce you to a somewhat odd passage of Scripture. It doesn't have the flair of a great miracle or the attention-grab of a fascinating parable. It is a more subtle moment that speaks an incredible truth that we need to face and own before we dive deeper into discipleship and walk with our students across to the other side of the river.

In Luke chapter 9, we are invited into three different conversations that Jesus had with three different people, all focused on the same thing (vv. 57–62). We sort of get to be a fly on the wall as Jesus helps these people to fully understand the commitment required of His disciples. We will call each of them prospective disciples. Let's meet them.

Prospect 1

I am sure you have met this kid. The new kid who is suddenly and incredibly eager for Jesus. The gospel has grabbed him, and there is no letting go—and do we ever celebrate! It's a prodigal son kind of moment. We support, encourage, and look for ways to use him as a leader. In fact, if we are honest, this initial enthusiasm is a dream come true, an answer to prayer for anyone leading youth. This kid is our first prospective disciple. Except Jesus doesn't seem to react the same way we do (vv. 57–58).

Jesus explains to this wannabe disciple that commitment means sacrificing his identity. Even the animals have a home, but Jesus does not, and consequently, neither will His disciples (v. 58). When most of us think of our homes, our comfortable beds, and all the comforts and convenience of indoor plumbing, we begin to question just what Jesus is asking. Is He really telling this prospect that he will not have a home? This certainly seems like an odd qualification for discipleship. But it makes you wonder: Would you still follow Jesus if homelessness was required?

The point Jesus is making here is much more significant than just homelessness. It's identity. One thing we have in common with the first-century world is that we are often defined by where we live, the jobs we have, and the families we belong to. Homelessness strips us of that identity. Without our homes, we are strangers, wanderers, and rejected. A disciple of Jesus needs to understand that following means living as a stranger and (potentially) suffering the same rejection He did. Rejection requires an incredible level of commitment—a level many of us simply don't have or perhaps cannot fathom. Jesus calls disciples to live as if they are homeless—not bound by the markings of our families, jobs, or neighborhoods. Living rejected and homeless means being committed to and trusting God, confident that our identity lies in the only place left—with Him.

Prospect 2

Let's meet the next student. She is faithful in coming to youth group, but does not seem to have a sense of urgency in living the life of a disciple. She has far too many more important things to be concerned with. Social media, the latest trends, Netflix, YouTube, and a persistent and paralyzing fear of missing out means there is little room left to commit much in the way of discipleship. Anytime there is a challenge to venture out to a mission trip, service project, or a chance to share her faith, there is always something that must come first. This is precisely the problem Jesus encountered with the second prospective disciple (vv. 59–60).

This call is similar to Jesus' call of John and his brother, who immediately left behind the family business with their father and followed Jesus. This man requested that before he followed, he would be permitted to take care of much-needed family affairs. The request seemed reasonable, given the priority family had in Jewish culture. Children were called to honor their father and mother and to provide proper care for the sick and dying, and funeral preparations held high importance. Certainly, Jesus would understand and respect the man's desire to do as culture and tradition demanded.

Jesus is not saying stop going to funerals for your loved ones or stop caring about your family. The meaning here is much greater than that. Jesus is talking about priorities. The kingdom is more important than the comforts of the world. The kingdom is more important than your family. Compare the choices—spread the gospel and give people a chance for eternal life or bury the dead?

How many times have we passed by the homeless man on the street corner, leaving him hungry because we have someplace to be? How many times have we opted to hang with friends rather than spend a Saturday serving food at the local shelter? We all have priorities and responsibilities to manage every day at every stage of life, but none of these responsibilities should ever supersede the work of Christ's kingdom.

Prospect 3

Now, for our final student. He has made the commitment. He put his faith in Christ. But shortly after, he realized that following Christ would mean no longer hanging out with his favorite group of friends, giving up the pornography on his computer, giving up the parties, drinking, and drugs, and coming clean to his parents. He continues to profess his faith in Jesus but is often pulled back into his old life and old habits. What might seem comfortable, what might seem to define his identity will eventually lead him down a road where sin wins. Real commitment means moving forward and not looking back. This is the plight of our final prospective disciple (vv. 61–62).

Even though this last request seems harmless and straightforward, it still serves as a warning. Throughout Scripture, looking back has not always been the best idea. For example, the nation of Israel looked back after they left Egypt. Often Israel wished they had not followed Moses across the sea—they even thought they would be better off in slavery. Lot's wife looked back on their way out from Sodom—which didn't work out all that well for her. Looking back suggests an attachment to what once was, the old life and the old values. Theologian Darrell Bock suggests that Jesus may be warning us that in the desire to bid farewell, you risk your heart remaining attached to the old life.[1] I think he is right. The busier, more connected, and complicated our lives become, the harder it is to shed our old identity steeped in the pull of the secular world and the desires of our flesh.

A commitment to follow Jesus is a promise to never look back. Nothing should ever be a higher priority than Christ or hinder your commitment to Him. Not friends, family, jobs, modern comforts, or social standing. What we are committed to speaks to what we desire. Commitment takes us beyond just what we know, into our deepest needs—it is as necessary as food and water. Commitment reveals what we love most—and what we love most, we worship.

Making It Stick

We all have excuses for not stopping for the homeless man on the corner, for not sharing our faith to our friends and family, for neglecting to do the right thing when called upon. We all have excuses for not following Jesus as He intends. Whether your motive is questionable, your priorities are skewed, or your uncertainty has you looking back, the mark of the disciple is not the emotionally-charged decision to like Jesus for what He can do for you. Deciding to follow Jesus is a moment, becoming a follower is a life-long commitment—a commitment to a new life, focused on His kingdom.

Followers of Jesus ultimately need to live a life that reflects God's image to the world. But what do we do about it? How can we help our students in their walk?

Creating space and time for practical conversations with students can present so many challenges. Those challenges are not just the excuses we create but also the distractions they contribute to the conversation. However, as we strive to reach this generation and the call to make disciples, we need to be prepared.

First, be transparent. When my house was near ruin, I didn't hide it from students or act like I had it all figured out. Far from it. I shared it. I wanted them to see that although I desperately wanted to see God at work and to have unwavering confidence, I had doubts. Whether it's the kids you lead and coach or your own children give them a little window into your world so they can see how to build a strong, lasting relationship with Jesus.

Second, encourage experiences that embrace and teach through the power of failure. Not the kind of experiences that will hurt them or tempt them to sin, but the kind that will teach— sometimes through success, but often through failure. I have never met a person who has not affirmed experience as the greatest of all teachers. But I have also met very few parents who allow that teacher into their home. Expect failure, embrace it, and be the first person to help students up when they fall.

Finally, teach and demonstrate what commitment looks like. Commitment is not a natural thing. It has to be taught. Start early. Show students the value of committing to teams, friends, family, and even church. Help them understand the cost of following Jesus and be there when the payment comes due.

None of this is automatic or a simple flip of the switch. It takes practice. Students will need your help to guide and mentor them through it.

Life will get hard; they will be tested. For Israel, the other side of the Jordan River may have been a deliverance of a long-awaited promise, but it was also ripe with incredible challenges from the surrounding cultures. They were tested time and again. And although they faltered and strayed from God, it was their commitment that continually brought them back and restored the relationship.

3

OVERLY DISTRACTED
AND COMPLETELY FOCUSED

*For victory in life, we've got to keep focused
on the goal, and the goal is Heaven.*

Lou Holtz

Focus. The epitome of concentration. It is sought after in nearly every area of life. Whether it's a career-defining meeting or college entrance exams, focus is critical. Even my eleven-year-old daughter is learning the hard lessons of focus as a young ballerina. Search the word *focus* at Amazon, and you'll find more than 50,000 books. For some it's even a matter of life and death. Surgeons, fighter pilots, astronauts, and even NASCAR drivers must maintain incredible focus and for long periods.

For a NASCAR driver, what might seem like hundreds of miles with nothing more than left turn after left turn is so much more. From the pit crew to the driver, every part of the team is in incredible shape and intensely focused. One wrong move could result in disaster—and it often does. In 2001, the iconic Dale Earnhardt was entering the final lap at the Daytona 500. A slight nudge on his rear bumper from another driver sent Earnhardt spinning down the middle of the track, slammed into by yet another car and into a wall at 155 mph, killing Earnhardt. At such a high speed there is no room for second guesses, mistakes, or even misfortune. While constant G-forces and torque on the driver's body take its toll for several hundred miles, he is required to think ahead, anticipate, and act decisively. All of which requires nearly supernatural amounts of focus.

Overly Distracted

The more we seem to understand the need for focus, the more we are becoming distracted.

The attention span of our students is now less than that of a goldfish; at least, that is according to a study done by Microsoft. In an article published by *Time* magazine, researchers interviewed more than 2,000 people and discovered most people lose their attention and concentration after about 8 seconds. A goldfish, however, can focus for a whopping 9 seconds. Surprising? Perhaps. But perhaps not. There are plenty who debate the accuracy of such a study. But consider for a moment your surroundings and what is competing for your attention as you begin this chapter. How many distractions pulled your attention away from reading? How many times did you check your phone? As I write this, I am sitting in a local coffee shop, and I can't help but look up from my screen to notice the delivery truck outside, the constant stream of people walking in and out, and even some of the conversations around me. My focus is broken over and over again. For most of us, maintaining attention and focus doesn't come naturally.

But our undivided focus is still the goal. It is the goal of every marketer, entertainer, and media outlet—to grab our attention and hold it for as long as possible. And they must do so inside a never-ending stream of stimulus begging for our attention. Just consider our entertainment. According to a study in 2010, the average duration for any given shot in a movie made before 1930 was about 12 seconds. Today that number is closer to 2.5 seconds. Meaning that every 2 seconds something on the screen changes—all designed to keep your attention.

Educators are following the same trend. Teachers from preschool to high school are regularly trained on how to keep changing delivery methods in any given lesson to adapt better to learning styles and attention spans. It seems with every technological advancement, faster communication, and unlimited streams of information, our attention is diverted into multiple competing directions. And there is no group more greatly affected than our students, and it's becoming increasingly dangerous to their faith in Christ.

Youth in an Age of Distraction

If you're of the GenX generation (born between 1961–1981), or older, you probably recognize names like Atari, Commodore, and the earliest versions of Nintendo. When we were introduced to the digital world for the first time, we marveled at what a few buttons could do to an object on the screen. Whether my grandmother's Pong or the local arcade's PacMan, we had the most unique experience in which we could enter a new world—briefly. At least until our quarters ran out or our mothers kicked us back outside. Distractions, yes. But they were harder to come by; they had to be sought out and certainly did not last.

For Millennials (born through 1995), that world changed dramatically—the internet was born. Suddenly the world became bigger and more accessible. The digital world began to draw closer. Just a few simple clicks and you could enter into a reality that seemed to have no boundaries. The space between the physical and the digital started to overlap. But unless you're some of the latest born in the Millennial generation, chances are you still had one computer and maybe even suffered through dial-up internet.

But what about GenZers (born after 1995)? I spoke with a pastor recently, and this is how he explained it to me. "When once kids played video games as another character, students today play them as themselves. It is no longer, 'look what I can make this guy do,' but 'look what I did!'" To me, this was a simple commentary on the digital reality of today's students and a window into the distractions they face. Thanks to the smartphone, there is no more going "online"; there is no more disconnecting, and there is no longer any difference between the physical and the digital. The world that we once had to enter into is the world our students were born into and cannot escape.

According to research conducted by Jean Twenge, psychology professor and generational expert at San Diego State University, high school seniors spend an average of more than two hours texting, two hours on the internet, more than an hour gaming and about half an hour on some type of video chat. That's six hours of leisure time distracted by some kind of media. Twenge writes, "Smartphones are unlike any other previous form of media, infiltrating nearly every minute of our lives, even where we are unconscious with sleep. While we are awake, the phone entertains, communicates, glamorizes." Very crudely, but simply put, students have better things to do than go to church. However, the fight for students' attention does not stop with smartphones and the internet. Our students are being inundated with every conceivable attraction pulling their engagement away from church activities and spiritual growth that extends far beyond the digital influence.

Recently the Barna Group did a comprehensive study on the intersection between faith and culture, much of which is focused on the rising generation. According to the study, busyness has become the latest family tradition. Nearly three-quarters of youth pastors surveyed cited students' busy lives as the number one hindrance in youth ministry. Yet parents did not seem all that concerned. Most felt their students had just about the right amount of activities and free time, essentially deprioritizing church and students' spiritual growth. Limited time, more activities, higher cultural demands, students' drive for financial success, and a genuine fear of missing out have paralyzed students leaving them with one foot in the door of our church buildings and one foot out. It's no wonder the top concern of youth pastors is students' lack of commitment to church and youth group activities.

In our desperate attempts to keep our students focused at church, we have upped the entertainment value, shortened sermons, and even made them less biblical and more motivational. All hoping to captivate the attention of our students, keep them coming, and if we are lucky, get them diving into devotionals, signing up for more mission trips, and even serving at church. But I wish I could say this was working. It's not. Sure, there is nothing wrong with having a great time worshipping Jesus, playing games, and even keeping messages succinct and to the point. But none of these adjustments are going to create the change necessary for our kids to redirect their focus and energy away from the countless digital distractions and toward Jesus and His purpose for their lives.

There are, however, adjustments you can make, which over time, will create lasting change and a bright future for our students.

Our Solution

The mantra of youth ministry is "entertain them, and they will come." Adopt the latest media trends, and sinners will repent. If my students can't tell the difference between the world and church, they might like Jesus more. I know, that sounds a little harsh and certainly not the case for every youth group, but I think it speaks to the desperate cry of every youth leader to find a way to reach students. No matter your role with students, you are forced to live in that tension between entering their world and creating a space for Jesus to consume their world.

In his book *You Are What You Love,* James K.A. Smith argues that youth ministry programs are primarily created out of fear that students will pack it up, leave the church, and leave their faith. Without providing attention-grabbing entertainment, students will run for the exit doors out of sheer boredom. Smith comments that in our efforts to be relevant, we have given the Bible—and thus, Jesus' commands in it—an inevitable irrelevance masked with the occasional and vague biblical reference but with sexier packaging. As if we are asking kids to "choke down medicine hidden inside a piece of candy." I think Smith is on to something here. What if, in our efforts to capture the attention of our youth and make Jesus relevant, we are actually making Him completely irrelevant?

Instead of succumbing to the distractions and the very things vying for the attention of our students, we need to ignore our tendency to jump on the bandwagon of the latest media trends and teach students what it would look like to live in light of the gospel that unsettles them from their daze caused by the world's countless distractions. We need Jesus to show us what it looks like to be laser-focused on Him, what it looks like to be so captivated by Him that their phones, social media, the internet, financial success, college entrance, travel sports teams, and social status no longer hold them hostage and steal their identity.

We need our students to be as focused as NASCAR drivers. Now I know Jesus didn't discuss NASCAR, but this is precisely the kind of focus required to cross the river.

What Jesus Says

Recently my friend got a new dog. Although the dog was really meant as a companion for his wife, it has become utterly obsessed with my friend. As he works throughout the day, the dog stares at him and follows him throughout the house—watching and analyzing every movement. This dog knows where my friend is during every waking hour. All of its attention is laser-focused.

A little creepy? Just a bit. But this ought to be our model for discipleship, so devoted to Jesus—fixated on learning Scriptures and putting them into action to become like Him—that we are entirely captivated by His every move. We cannot be disciples of Jesus if we are not focused on Him. We cannot be followers of Him if we keep getting distracted by something else.

In Christian circles, we often refer to the cost of discipleship. Espousing the belief that we must be willing to give up anything—and perhaps everything—as an act of devotion to following Jesus (Luke 14:33). Jesus even tells a huge crowd traveling with Him that they can't be disciples unless one hates their mother and father (14:26) and they must bear their own cross and follow

Him (v. 27). A bit later, in Luke's gospel, a young ruler inquired about discipleship and eternal life. Jesus' response was much the same. "Sell everything you have and give it to the poor, then come follow me" (Luke 18:22). Are these really the qualifications for discipleship? Are we really telling our students that to follow Jesus, one needs to seek out suffering, hate their parents, and be completely poor?

Not in the least. Jesus is speaking to the distractions which haunted the people in the first-century. Wealth, status, and even family obligations could all drive their attention from Jesus. His words served as a clear warning: guard yourself against the desires for wealth and anything else that may lead to idolatry. You can't serve both God and money (Matt. 6:24; Luke16:13). Our attraction to shiny new things risks the life that Jesus is calling us to. A life of discipleship is a life which demands everything that you are.

If you have ever made any attempt to create life change, then you know there is no automatic switch or magic formula. And unless you're some kind of motivational anomaly, you have likely failed in many of those attempts. Don't worry, I won't remind you of your last New Year's resolution. Now just imagine what young Christians deal with every day. If we want confidence that our students will carry their faith and grow in Christ throughout their lives, then we need to embrace the process of sanctification and our partnership with the Holy Spirit. But what does that process look like? How do we make Jesus' words stick and help our youth become better followers while navigating endless distractions?

Making It Stick

"What do you mean she doesn't have a phone?" That was the reaction of the cashier at the local Target. She was in utter disbelief that my wife and I did not see the urgent need to supply my eleven-year-old daughter with unlimited access to the digital world.

Many of her friends do have some kind of smart device, and we have had the subsequent "my friends have them, why can't I" conversation during more than one family dinner.

However, my reasoning is much more complex than not giving my kids access to a completely unfiltered world. Although that is part of it, it's more about developing the right kinds of habits at the earliest possible age. Which is also where I believe keeping our attention on Jesus and not being dazzled by distractions begins. Which is precisely what captivates a young, developing teenage brain.

A teenager's brain is hardwired to learn. Simultaneously more powerful and more vulnerable than any other point in their lives. Every experience etching in neural pathways solidifying knowledge, habits, and even addictions. The bigger the experience, or the more an activity is repeated, the deeper that pathway is etched, making it harder and harder over time to change behaviors. Everything our kids are exposed to creates an effect—intended or not.

The distractions surrounding our students' digital reality are literally causing a biochemical reaction initiating the effects of addiction—every notification, like, share or retweet causes a rise in dopamine levels further feeding the addiction. Students are not just captivated by the world offered in the new age of media, they are addicted to it and experiencing cognitive overload. Let me offer two quick and very doable solutions that can make an immediate impact.

First, build better habits into your students. The solution lies in the habits we instill in our children and youth from the earliest of ages. I want my eleven-year-old to first develop the habits of prayer and daily Bible reading, long before she is introduced to an uninterrupted and unfiltered online world. Our brains are always looking for a way to use the least possible amount of energy. So I want her to know the value of silence and being still before God before she is required to navigate the ongoing, endless noise of our media-saturated world. Just like bad habits and addictions, at a young age, the right habits can carve neurological paths in their brains that become very hard to break—spiritual habits which draw them closer to Christ to become more like Him. Our minds are powerful and precisely the reason Paul tells us to be transformed in the renewing of our minds (Rom. 12:2).

Think about the last time you learned a new skill. Maybe playing an instrument, or perhaps painting. For me, when I was a young athlete, I prided myself on being able to shoot a basketball right and left-handed. I would spend hours in my driveway practicing left-handed layups and free throws. Carefully and meticulously teaching my muscles how to move and shoot the ball properly. I knew when I would have it right—once it no longer felt awkward in my left hand. I knew I would have it when my brain didn't know the difference between shooting with my right versus my left hand. When we think of building spiritual habits, the same principle applies. It will feel odd and awkward. But careful repetition will create sound spiritual habits that will feel as natural as tying our shoes.

Second, help your students be perfect. I know what you're thinking: nobody's perfect. But that's not the kind of perfect I am talking about here. It's what Jesus says toward the beginning of the Sermon on Mount in Matthew chapter 5: "Be perfect, as my Father in Heaven is perfect" (Matt. 5:48). The word we translate as perfect is the ancient Greek word, *telos*. It conveys the idea of something or someone's end goal or purpose. At this moment, Jesus is forcing us to consider why we exist. What are we here for? What is our purpose?

Telos sets the stage for the mission God has given His people and sets the stage for what is on the other side of the river and what life will look like once we are across. Our intended goal is Christlikeness. It is to be our obsession, what captivates our attention, drives our ambition, and animates routine life with renewed excitement.

Helping our youth find how they fit into God's mission and purpose for their lives helps create a deeper sense of focus and helps prevent being sidetracked by the lure of countless distractions. Our goal as leaders of youth in every capacity ought to be helping our students discover their passions, their purpose, and their gifts—and more importantly—how they can be used to advance the gospel in their schools and communities. Our goal should be to help students use every available resource and tool to build the kingdom and move them closer to God's intended *telos* for their lives.

We need to teach our students to live in such a way that reflects the gospel so perfectly it awakes the church from its daze transfixed on the blue glow of their smartphones. Doing so will help students rethink how they participate in culture and engage it with the gospel. Jesus was not teaching that things of the world are inherently evil—that we should disavow all earthly things. However, the Bible makes it clear that earthly treasures do become evil when they captivate our attention and distract us from our *telos*, that those things become idols and replace our need for Christ.

We cannot serve both God and money or video games, Netflix, YouTube, Instagram, or every like or share that provides the illusion of self-worth only God can provide. What we often fail to realize is that our youth do not intuitively know how to use the things of this world to glorify God. We have to teach them. Our students don't know how to self-regulate dangerously, distracting entertainment or social media. We have to guide them in developing godly lasting habits which create spiritual growth.

Conclusion

Joshua told Israel to keep an eye on the ark and to watch the priests. When they move, you move. In the meantime, consecrate yourself. In other words, pay attention and get ready. Don't miss what God is about to do. Joshua was telling the Israelites to be focused.

Imagine Israel so distracted they missed crossing the river, missed the miracle, and missed the promise. Our students are far more distracted than any previous generation. Their attention is literally being pulled in every conceivable direction. It's not enough to simply walk with them in their journey of discipleship while their faces are buried into their smartphones or sit with students as they feed their gaming addiction in hopes we stumble on a Jesus conversation. We have to intentionally teach our youth—from an early age—how to steer through an increasingly toxic world. Teaching our students to focus on Christ will ensure they don't miss the life God has promised on the other side of the water.

Commitment is essential, but focus moves commitment forward.

4

GREAT FAITH OR
SAFE FAITH?

*Faith is taking the first step even when
you don't see the whole staircase.*

Martin Luther King, Jr.

Over the years, I have had many great students, but Katie was exceptional. Smart, articulate, and a natural leader. Her dad was a pastor at the local church, and there was every indication that in some fashion Katie would also devote her life to ministry. But despite her strong Christian upbringing, vibrant youth ministry, and even the strong Christian community at our Christian school, there was something drastically missing. When asked to describe her belief and understanding of Jesus, she remarked that Jesus was "a great teacher, a sort of divine compass for us to model." On the surface, it appeared her perception of Jesus was spot on. However, when I spoke about Jesus being the only means to the Father (John 14:6) or affirmed Jesus' authority over every aspect of our lives, she would often retort that those passages or parables were outdated and irrelevant. Katie insisted that the Bible's *version* of Jesus was far too ancient for a modern world.

But Katie is a Millennial. Today's GenZ students have an even greater challenge to live out a traditional evangelical Christian faith in the twenty-first century world they inhabit. It is far more common for GenZers to see discipleship as a personalized buffet of ideas, church attendance as optional, and a more generalized belief in a higher power commonly known as "God." Students may confess a belief of sorts in Jesus, but they don't necessarily believe one has to follow the Bible in a literal sense.

Instead, be a good person and have good intentions. Which of course, eliminates any need to share one's faith—something Gen-Zers are generally opposed to.[1] So, where then does this leave our students' faith when we consider questions of doubt and morality and issues of identity? Rightfully, our students are making every effort to love others unconditionally. Not only do they live in a more diverse culture than any previous generation, but they also embrace it.

If Katie was one of the brightest students I ever had, Mary was likely the most loving. As one of the oldest of GenZ, Mary frequently wrestled with reconciling biblical commands with loving others like Jesus. I know what you're thinking. How hard can that be? Jesus loved everyone, ate with tax collectors and sinners. He was even repeatedly questioned by the religious authorities regarding His behavior. But for Mary, the narrow path was far too narrow. As I taught on topics like discipleship, theology, and the nature of sin, she would mutter under her breath, "not my Jesus." For Mary, loving others meant that morals needed to be flexible. Love and acceptance of everyone called for an unapologetic affirmation of their behavior.

Would You Rather?

My family loves to play silly games at dinner time. We often ask questions about our favorite parts of the day or best part of someone else in the family. That sort of thing. One of our favorites is the game "Would you rather?" It is the challenge of asking another person to choose between two things they potentially love. For example, one of my daughters recently asked me, "Would you rather play with us all day, or go to work?" A bit of a trick question, but the fun is watching them try and dig a little deeper into who we are and what we love. I think our students are playing the same game with Jesus. Treating Jesus as though they have to choose between following Jesus and loving others. And given a choice, loving others wins out every time. For many of our students, loving others means either ignoring Jesus altogether or creating an alternative Jesus more palatable for the rising generation.

It is as if the next generation is attempting to create a faith that loves but without Jesus at the center. But such an idea has dire consequences. Without Jesus at the center, what need is there for sharing their faith in Him? Without Jesus at the center, how do they navigate things like morality, evil, heaven, and hell? As we have seen so far, our students are facing a long list of obstacles which actively threaten their pursuit of an authentic relationship with Jesus. If it's not our increasingly post-Christian and pluralistic culture, it is often churches with poor theology and a weak gospel, or simply the challenges of being a teenager in twenty-first century culture.[2] For Katie and Mary these challenges meant really loving Jesus without any intention of following Him. It meant belief and spirituality without discipleship. It meant the gospel is good advice rather than good news.

Pastor and journalist John S. Dickerson, in his book *Hope of Nations*, comments that "Many young Christians have placed their faith in Christ, but they are still thinking from a post-truth paradigm which has been deeply indoctrinated into them by the culture."[3] Therefore, if we have any hope in guiding the next generation to a life of biblical discipleship, we need to uncover what it truly means to have genuine faith and completely submit to Jesus' authority. We have seen what commitment looks like and explored the call to keep our eyes locked on Him. But what does faith look like when life happens, when the storms come, the questions arise, and even doubt creeps in?

What Were They Thinking?

Author and religion historian at Boston University, Stephen Prothero, did a comprehensive study on how Jesus became a bit of a national icon morphed into nearly every nationality, gender, race, even hobby. "Jesus has been depicted as black and white, male and female, straight and gay, a socialist and a capitalist, a pacifist and a warrior, a Ku Klux Klansman and a civil rights agitator."[4] All of which points us to a Jesus that closer resembles an expression of our own hopes and fears, ourselves, and our nation.[5]

But such a misunderstanding of Jesus is not new. Even the closest followers of Jesus often misunderstood the nature of Jesus' authority and the kind of faith He required. The very notion of the Jewish Messiah was never God incarnate, much less a third person of the Holy Trinity. The Messiah was a Davidic ruler, anointed by God to conquer any foreign nation ruling over Israel and reestablish God's people as the rightful king in their own land. Yet throughout the Gospels, we get a front-row seat as first-century Palestine discovers they had short-changed Jesus all along. We have the privilege of seeing, first hand, the disciples' evolution of thought as they peeled back the layers about what following Jesus would mean now and for the rest of their lives.

To illustrate this, let's uncover a few layers to discover how this thought process flowed and what it can mean for raising up the next generation of disciples.

Layer one

It became known as the Minneapolis Miracle. The 2018 NFC divisional playoff game. The winner advances to the NFC Championship game—one game away from the Super Bowl. The Minnesota Vikings, down by just one, ball in hand, stood about sixty yards from the end zone and at best, twenty yards from a field goal attempt. But with no timeouts left, a win was unlikely. Minnesota quarterback Case Keenum connects with wide receiver Stefon Diggs for the unlikely touchdown to win the game. Now, if you're a New Orleans Saints fan, you likely thought, with ten seconds left, the game was over. All the Saints had to do was tackle Diggs in bounds. The clock would expire and game over. Instead, the impossible happened. Saints fans were stunned.

Even if you're not a football fan, you probably get what I am talking about. Pick any other sport—even politics, entertainment, or the news. Moments where jaws dropped, minds raced, thoughts completely frozen in time, stunned at what had just happened. A moment likely to never be forgotten.

I might be slightly overplaying this, but this is how I imagine the crowd would have been like after Jesus delivered the Sermon on the Mount (Matt. 5–7). Fresh on the scene, Jesus announced the arrival of the coming kingdom in an incredible authoritative style. So much so, that when he finished, the crowds were amazed at His teaching, "because he taught as one who had authority and not as their teachers of the law" (Matt.7:28–29). The crowd was speechless. They had never seen someone who spoke the way Jesus did. I'm sure it was a moment they would never forget. This is the first layer. It's like we have reached the summit where we discover Jesus is something far different than we had imagined and His words mean more than we ever thought possible. But this is only the beginning. We have yet to uncover Jesus' full authority and what it means for the church.

Layer two

A few years ago, my wife and I had the opportunity to take a brief trip to Atlanta without the kids. We hadn't been on any kind of trip without the kids since before we had them. So, although work-related, we looked forward to our mini-weekend getaway. I fly on a somewhat regular basis. My wife, on the other hand, hadn't in years. So the whole process from timing at the airport, security, baggage, what lines to stand in, when and where, I have down to a precise science. As we progressed through the air travel process, little did I realize that there was a growing degree of tension and anxiety in my wife. I found out once we boarded the plane.

Sure, she was nervous, but she told me she was fine. Until the plane began to taxi to the runway. I was just relaxing in my seat, half paying attention to the flight attendant, concerned with more important things—like what movie I planned to watch. The second we broke from the jetway, her face went ghost white, she grabbed my hand, cutting off circulation and leaving grip marks. From that moment, every noise, bit of turbulence, or sudden change in altitude had her terrified. I am not sure what bothered her more, her anxiety, or the fact that I didn't have a care in the world. It's the unknown. It can be terrifying.

So let's turn a few pages in Matthew's Gospel. Seeking to get away from the crowds, Jesus got into a boat, and of course, the disciples followed Him. Jesus and His disciples were in a boat relaxing (Matt. 8:23–27). They sailed along, and Jesus fell asleep. A huge storm flared up in a matter of moments. The massive change in elevation created (and still creates) unpredictable weather patterns on the Sea of Galilee. Keep in mind, most of the disciples were fishermen. They were seasoned veterans, used to this lake and aware of its crazy weather. But the storm was so bad they were certain they were going to die. So naturally, they woke up Jesus.

With just a word, Jesus stopped the storm and saved the day. Let's be real; this is Jesus we are talking about. Should we be all that surprised or even impressed? Even the disciples expected Jesus to do something. They had faith—even genuine faith in Jesus. But what we learn from this moment is that their faith, although genuine, was limited, and they were accused of having little faith (v. 26). But why does Jesus accuse His disciples of little faith just because they were afraid? It's because the disciples weren't fully aware of Jesus' authority and power.[6]

Once the winds died down, the waves vanished into the sea, the disciples looked to each other in amazement and wondered "Who is this guy?" "Where did he come from?" Up to this point, the disciples, from the moment they were called to follow Jesus had spent every waking moment with their Teacher. They heard about the kingdom; they saw Jesus assert His authority over the Law of Moses; they saw His power over disease as He healed leprosy, paralysis, and even demon possession. So what was the big deal here? Their limited faith left them speechless and dumbfounded by the reality of Jesus' true identity and mission. Now consider your own faith and the faith you are imparting to the students you lead. This is layer two. Is your faith producing the right perception of Jesus to your students? Are they learning to have great faith or safe faith?

One final layer

When I taught apologetics for high school students, my favorite assignment was their final project. They had to take all their knowledge and skills developed over the semester, find a non-Christian, and engage in a conversation about life and faith with them—intending on introducing the gospel. Every student, every semester, every year, was absolutely terrified—at least at first. You could see it in their eyes as I introduced the project at the beginning of each semester. Most students, by the end, felt prepared and did a great job—except Bobby.

Bobby came from a non-Christian family, but loved Jesus, went to church with friends, took advantage of as many camps and activities as possible. He was a good student and great kid, considering the odds at home were stacked against him. The most natural thing for him to do was to interview one of his family members. But he made it clear that family was off the table. I didn't push but told him we would pray about it. And we did. A lot. And the more we prayed, the more he felt that was what God was asking of him. But in his mind, this was entirely impossible. Especially at that moment. There had been unusually high tension in the home. The timing just felt all wrong. But neither Bobby or I could shake the nudging we were both feeling from the Spirit.

I shared with him Peter's experience of walking on water (Matt.14:23–36). If you have spent any time in the Bible, you are likely familiar with the passage. If not, I encourage you to take a minute and read the whole story. Go ahead, I'll wait.

Peter and the other eleven are back out on the Sea of Galilee in the middle of the night. Off in the distance, they see a figure walking on the water. Naturally, they were terrified, thinking it's a ghost, until Jesus calmed their fears and let them know it was He. But not until Peter proposed to jump out of the boat and walk out to Jesus. So to be clear, Peter asked Jesus to allow Him to do the impossible. But the minute the winds picked up and the waves got just a bit too big, Peter lost focus and started to sink, crying out to Jesus for help.

Here is that final layer. I reminded Bobby that the Christian life is filled with moments when we are asked to do what seems like the impossible. That notion of being able to do all things through Christ comes when we fix our eyes on Jesus and do what we can to ignore the darkness, the wind, and the waves. But when doubt creeps in, we have the encouragement of Jesus' words and the Spirit's power. Bobby overcame his fear. And although his family didn't fall down on their knees and give their lives over to Jesus (although that would have been cool), they were open to the conversation and gained a greater appreciation for what their son believed and why.

Making It Stick

These three examples provide for us great insight into the effect culture can have on how we see Jesus. As Jesus entered the first-century scene, He was confronted head-on with many of the standard cultural norms—especially in terms of religious identity. Even as Jesus' closest followers grew to know Him at a deeper level, when faced with difficulty, it became easier to rely on themselves, their knowledge, and their experience, rather than the authority of Jesus. They had heard His teaching, seen His miracles, prayed His prayers, but when difficulty arose, they still couldn't figure out what to expect from Him.

As youth leaders, pastors, and parents, we often forget that we preach forgiveness and the beauty of following Jesus without realizing that for many of them we are inviting them into a life that seems entirely impossible. We are sending them into a world loudly proclaiming the doctrines of secularism. In *Meet Generation Z,* James Emery White observes, "In our world, increasing numbers of people lead their lives without any sense of needing to look to a higher power, to something outside of themselves. Leaders of science and commerce, education and politics—regardless of their personal views—do not tend to operate with any reference to a transcendent truth, much less a God."[7] These are the origins of our post-Christian culture. And the younger the generation, the more post-Christian they become. Meaning that while many Christian students are still attending churches, reading their Bibles, and participating in youth group, the role of religion in public life and the cultural authority the church once held has been almost entirely eliminated—creating far too many avenues of escape and means of distraction.

So what happens when the storms come? What happens when secularism doesn't have an answer for evil? Where do we turn when human wisdom can't seem to bring enough hope to the world? When our students don't fully surrender to the authority of Jesus, they are left crippled by their own fears and doubts. They might be willing to step into the water but lack the spiritual strength to make it all the way across.

So what's the solution? I have two.

Put the Bible at the center.

I had a unique privilege while teaching in Christian schools. They were all interdenominational. Which means that at any given moment, I had a classroom full of Baptists, Pentecostals, Lutherans, a few Catholics, non-denominationalists, Methodists, and even a few atheists. Nearly a hundred churches represented from almost every tradition, doctrinal formation, liturgy, and youth ministry design. Some students wanted to focus on deep discussion involving complex theological positions. Others wanted nothing more than to sit around the room, hold hands, and pray. I had parents who thought I treated the Bible too much like a textbook, and other parents who accused me of taking the Bible too lightly. Some wanted academics, others devotional time. You get the idea.

These wide-ranging differences taught me a valuable lesson. Stick to Scripture. It was so tempting to teach these students all *about* the Bible and all *about* Jesus, but while they all differed in tradition, they nearly all viewed Jesus the same—a great moral teacher. More and more young Christians see Jesus less as a historical person, less as the incarnate Son of God, and more as an idealistic icon leveraged for personal morals and social justice. A perception derived from Moralistic Therapeutic Deism—treating Jesus as a moral therapist. A love for Jesus absent of discipleship.

It took me a few years, but my solution was simple. I taught them who Jesus was and how we ought to follow Him through the Bible—and only the Bible. I think Dickerson has it exactly right: "Incoming younger Christians who sincerely love Jesus will not have been taught the importance of the infallibility of Scripture or related documents that elevate the Word of God as the authority for all we do and believe."[8] The more we ignore the Jesus of the Bible, the closer we are to ignoring our faith.

Take a minute and ask your students about the authority and infallible nature of the Bible. If the Bible is not perfect, then we don't have a Jesus who can speak with absolute authority, stop storms, or call us to do the impossible. Who then are we following exactly? What reason do I have for even believing in Jesus, worshipping Him, or introducing others to Him? Culture has taught us that the Jesus of the Bible is too harsh, too bigoted, too hateful, and no longer relevant for today's audience. Therefore, we need not take the Bible so literally and only use it as a general guide when it fits our current cultural climate and emotional needs.

However, recently, I came across some fascinating research conducted by the Center for Bible Engagement. They interviewed more than 200,000 people from eight to eighty years old, from twenty countries, and more than seventy-five denominations.

They discovered that just by reading the Bible four times a week, a person's life could change radically. They determined that someone who engages the Bible four or more times a week is 228 percent more likely to share their faith with others, 407 percent more likely to memorize Scripture, 59 percent less likely to view pornography, and 30 percent less likely to struggle with loneliness.[9] The conclusion: *Scripture changes lives.* More specifically, *the Jesus in Scripture changes lives.*

Stop mowing the lawn.

From the moment I entered student ministry to the moment I held my oldest daughter for the first time—even today, I constantly battle my tendency to mow down every conceivable obstacle to ensure success in every area of their lives. Like I said earlier, if Millennials were recipients of helicopter parents, GenZ kids have lawnmower parents. And it is a trend that is setting our students up for failure.

Clearing away the obstacles in the path of our students will damage their faith. It will impair their ability to persevere and their ability to grow in Christ. It will prevent them from ever walking on water. The kind of faith we hope for our youth is the kind that is refined and tested. The sort of faith birthed out of perseverance, trials, and testing is the kind that is proved genuine, purified by fire, and brings us closer to Christ (1 Peter 1:6–9). Let me give you two quick ways this can happen.

First, our students need the great lessons taught by experience and trial and error. We expect pain in so many other areas of life. If you play sports, you expect sore muscles; learn to play guitar, and the strings will make your fingers bleed; study any academic discipline long enough and you will experience mental exhaustion. Why would faith be treated any differently?

Second, learn alternative viewpoints. The best time to expose students to other viewpoints and ideas is before they head off to college—allow the presence of good mentors, teachers, and parents to help students process those ideas inside a biblical framework.

Conclusion

As far as I know, Katie and Mary are not currently chasing after Jesus. They are not attending church or involved in any means of advancing the gospel in their communities. I often wonder where their faith would be if they'd had the right perception of Jesus— one drawn from the pages of the Bible instead of their own version. Their need for faith was entirely dependent on their circumstances and how culture instructed them. Eventually that need was replaced by a much easier doctrine of secularism. Their version of Jesus gave them safe faith.

Jesus doesn't ask us to play it safe; He is calling us into the river. In fact, He is calling us to walk on water. And no matter the storms, no matter the cultural climate, helping our students fix their eyes on Jesus will give them the strength they need to drive out fear and grow as disciples for a great faith.

5
LEAVING SIN BEHIND

*The best time to plunge into the deeper spiritual life
is when you are a young Christian and have enthusiasm
and can form deep-seated habits.*

A.W. Tozer

Back in 2018 the popular song *This Is Me*, from the movie *The Greatest Showman*, was featured at the Oscars to a worldwide audience. Performed by the somewhat unknown actress and singer Keala Settle, the performance brought Hollywood to its feet and the song was quickly launched into Western pop culture. The song reverberated as an anthem of acceptance and love for all, a battle cry for those who feel the weight of trying to fit in.

The song and many others like it teach powerful lessons of acceptance and the importance of being the best version of yourself. Who you are, as you are, and how you are is exactly how you ought to be. No one should tell you otherwise.

I have to admit, I do love the song—not to mention the movie; it's one of our family favorites. It's the kind of song that fills your soul with adrenaline—a sense of pride and empowerment. I would be lying if I said we didn't crank up the volume and join the kids in trying to imitate the dance moves. But the song's message is a clear echo of our culture's post-truth doctrine. Despite its uplifting message, *This Is Me* and others like it preach the denial of human depravity.

If you are a part of older generations, you might not see the immediate connection. There was a time, a little more than a generation ago, when most everyone considered the human heart to be deceitful above all things and beyond cure (Jer. 17:9). The

Western world had a firm grasp on mankind's depravity and the moral compass by which we understood God's ideal for humanity.[1] In other words, there was no argument about whether one was a sinner. The sin nature of people still held the majority opinion. However, today, that is no longer true.

There was a time when preachers like Billy Graham could take the stage and passionately and effectively remind his audience that they were sinners in need of repentance and the grace of God through Christ. In the modern world, a declaration of another's sins could be perceived as an act of intolerance and aggression.

The overwhelming narrative is that people are inherently good. If we are already good—good just the way we are—then what need is there for the Christian's effort to be like Christ? What need is there to be an imitator of God (Eph. 5:1)? Without the recognition of sin and depravity, what do we do with spiritual growth in our students? Where do sanctification and living the resurrected life take center stage? Whether we realize it or not—or admit it or not—the church and the Christian home have placed spiritual growth on the back-burner.

GenZ students may consider themselves spiritual, but unless they are incredibly engaged with their church, most teens don't consider spiritual growth to hold much importance or priority—at least in the context of church.[2] Whether it is the rise of moral relativism or the disinclination toward organized religion, our students see the notion of holiness and righteousness as an intolerant attempt to elevate one belief over another. Something modern culture simply won't tolerate. The relativistic nature of Western culture is making it increasingly difficult for students to leave sin behind, to pursue radical discipleship, to live completely surrendered to the lordship of Jesus, and walk in obedience toward *te-los*—the pursuit of purpose.

What you might not realize is that far too often the gospel is realigned with cultural messages like *This Is Me*. This incredibly well-written and well performed song misses a vital piece of what it means to follow Christ. Stopping at "Jesus loves me as I am" is only half of the story. Although the beauty of the gospel is that there is no behavioral prerequisite to the family of God. Anyone who would recognize their own sin and call on the name of Jesus is immediately and unconditionally welcomed in. But biblical discipleship, the kind that not only crosses the Jordan River but successfully reflects the image and glory of God on the other side, requires the resurrected life—a life in constant pursuit of holiness. Our cry to Jesus is to save us and change us, not to declare *This Is Me.*

But if we want our students to turn from sin, grow spiritually, and pursue holiness, we need to first understand how our culture's perception of sin has drastically changed, what we can learn from Scripture, and how to filter that information into how we speak into the lives of our youth.

How You Are Versus Who You Are

I am certain you have noticed it. If you turn on the television, browse the Internet, watch the news, listen to music, or go pretty much anywhere in public, you'll notice that the notion of sin is rapidly losing its place at the table and in the cultural conversation. As I mentioned earlier, the line we draw between what is sin and what is not is a constantly moving target. With the arrival of every new generation, we lay aside more and more sin, quietly accepting and normalizing it. For our students, ignoring or standing against these new social norms could result in dire consequences—most notably a public sense of disapproval, social media shaming, and ostracism from certain social groups. Our culture is insistent that morality and sin are a matter of choice driven by the gratification of felt needs.[3] Therefore, acting according to my own felt needs eliminates another's right to tell me if that choice is either right or wrong—all the while ignoring or dismissing the potential consequences. This is what is called *Moral Intuitionism*, meaning that students are taught to believe that they can know what is right and wrong by attending to subjective feelings or intuitions that they sense within themselves.[4]

Let's be clear. This sort of thing is not isolated to our students' schools, activities, or other secular areas of their lives. It's happening in our churches too. There are (at least) two specific and incorrect perceptions that are being passed down to our students. While much of it may originate from culture, historically, the church has not done a great job of balancing the task of defining sin and pursuing holiness—and doing so from a place of grace and truth.

Recently I attended a gathering of youth leaders from around the country. As I spent time scheduling lunches, attending sessions, and meeting new people, I kept hearing one resounding concern on the minds of these youth workers: sin and identity. Spend just a few minutes with youths, and this concern will come as no surprise. What caught me off guard was some of the advice given from some of the most respected youth ministry leaders. They said that to show students love, we must accept them for who they are—even if that means violating commonly held beliefs about sin. Essentially cheering them on as they declare, "This is me."

For example, one of the most important conversations in youth ministry is sexual identity. The Lesbian, Gay, Bisexual, Transgender, and Queer (LGBTQ) community has successfully infused into Western culture the narrative that one's sexual desires are inherent to their identity. Instead of a chosen behavior subject to a specific standard of morality, sexuality is no different than race, nationality, or even one's height—because you can't change how you were born. Therefore, they are normalizing it into the same categories as civil rights. So it would seem almost natural for the church's response to be one of acceptance and affirmation, which is precisely what these youth leaders were advocating— loving our students by affirming their sexual desires because it is fused to their identity and, therefore, fused to how God must have created them. For these leaders—and many others in youth ministry—the best means of loving our students is to allow sin to go unchecked in hopes they might hear the gospel.

Christians all over the globe struggling with sin issues like same-sex attraction and gender dysphoria have unapologetically declared that sexual attraction is at the core of human identity. Christopher Yuan, in his book, *Holy Sexuality and the Gospel*, perfectly captures the issue. We have shifted the conversation surrounding sin from *how* I am to *who* I am and from experience to ontology—the nature or understanding of how we come to know the nature of our being.[5]

Sin Is Not a Thing

I remember as a kid how I would like to steal. I would ride my bike over to the local convenience store. Okay, really it was a liquor store. But among the countless shelves of wine and whiskey and endless rows of fridges stocked with beer was plenty of candy and my preferred beverage of black cherry flavored New York Seltzer. I would pick out what I wanted for the day, set my stuff on the counter, and if the clerk ever took his eyes off of me (remember these were the days before surveillance cameras), I would swipe the closest thing within reach. Usually baseball cards or Swedish Fish. I loved the rush. I *knew* it was wrong. That's why it was so thrilling. In fact, I don't ever remember a conversation with my parents or teachers about whether or not stealing was wrong. I knew it was. In fact, that was the point. Most of my conversations were spent trying to convince someone that it wasn't me so I could avoid getting in trouble and continue to steal.

Today, more and more, it's like sin is not a thing—our chosen behaviors are linked to ontology. As a teacher, I saw it take root even in the smallest of ways. Each morning making my way to my classroom required some very strategic footwork. Not only did I have to dodge the mass waves of students making their way about the school, but I had to step over the endless rows of students sitting in the hallway astutely working on homework. I was always so impressed and proud that these students worked so hard, worked in community, and helped each other. That is until we as a staff realized what was actually happening.

They were cheating.

But here is the thing—unlike my affinity for stealing Swedish Fish, these students didn't think they were cheating. Once we realized what was going on, I pulled a few students into my office and simply asked for an explanation. To make sure I got the best possible explanation, I went right for the best students, the most honest and trustworthy students. But despite my best interrogation methods, I couldn't seem to get them to admit to cheating. Because according to them they did not see it as cheating. It didn't matter what the instructions on their homework said, the clear statement in the school's handbook, or that all of their papers were identical. They truly didn't see the harm or immorality of their actions. Working on their homework in this fashion was part of *who* they were and had nothing—in their minds—to do with *how* they were sinning.

I know this is just a simple example, and if you're like me, you're wondering how in the world is that even possible. Its common sense, right? Perhaps not. Welcome to the world of moral relativism. And the effects are being felt in more important areas of life than student homework assignments. Sin is up for grabs, internally defined, and governed by emotion. The lessons of "you only live once" (YOLO), "follow your heart," and "you be you" all originate from a post-truth ideology and drive the idea that what you feel is the only true measurement of what is true. It's dramatically affecting how we disciple our students. No matter the degree of sin, if we don't recognize our own fallenness, then we have no need for Jesus and, therefore, no reason to pursue holiness.

Forgiveness Rules All

There are few things greater than seeing your own child come to you genuinely seeking forgiveness. Not the begrudging, "I'm sorry" said out of obligation; but that moment where you pat yourself on the back for a parenting job well done. As Christian parents, we jump at the opportunity to show them that extreme love of God—that no matter the offense, we love completely and unconditionally.

Until the same offense happens again and again and again. Sure, the apologies keep coming, and you think you see the sincerity and genuine remorse. But what's missing is repentance. In a moment of parenting weakness, I blurted out to my oldest daughter—after an annoying repeat offense, "I am sick of hearing, 'I'm sorry.' Stop saying it!" Like I said, not my finest moment. But I am sure you can relate to the frustration. Imagine the story of the Prodigal Son (Luke 15:11–32) ending much differently. Instead of a grand party for the youngest son's return—the celebration and joy of the lost one returning home, repenting, and setting a new course for life—the son waits a few months or years and repeats the story over again. The same behaviors with the same result, looking for the same forgiveness.[6]

What might seem ridiculous is not far off from what many students are taught. "Jesus loves me just as I am" is the feel-good tagline for many. And perhaps rightfully so. The church works tirelessly to convey the message that salvation is not transactional. There is nothing we have to do to earn it, no benchmarks to hit before we qualify, and no rituals to perform to be worthy of it. Jesus does in fact say, "Come as you are." But that is only where salvation begins. There is more. Following Jesus is putting sin aside—leaving it behind. It is the acceptance of the gift of forgiveness *and* the pursuit of the life of holiness.

Chasing Holiness

While culture reverberates the message of "you be you," the gospel requires you to be better than you—to be like Christ. The life that God requires is one that has died to sin (Rom. 6:2) and has been reborn and resurrected into a new life (Rom. 6:4). This is precisely the point the apostle Paul is making in his letter to the Romans. Paul is addressing the covenant faithfulness of God to deliver the promise made to Israel to restore what was once broken since sin entered the world. Jesus made this possible through His obedient death on the cross and resurrection three days later. Paul makes it clear that the entire scope of God's promise, the hope of creation, rests in the resurrection. The resurrection becomes the answer not just to sin itself, but to its consequences.[7] If there is no sin for us to be worried about, then what did Jesus resurrect for? What need would we have to be a new creation, reborn into the family of God?

Our slavery to sin no longer binds us, and therefore death's mastery over us is no more (Rom. 6:9). To be "in Christ" means that we are already seated with Christ in the heavenly places (Eph. 2:6) and yet remain here in the body. We are justified in Christ, reconciled to God, and have put on the new self, continually being renewed each day in the likeness of God, our original design and purpose (Col. 3:10). All of this constitutes life now, and yet we look forward to the future life to come.

As a new creation, we of course, cannot stay as we are. If sin has been put to death with Christ, and in baptism we have been raised, then the deeds of our flesh must be eliminated as we become more holy. Our body is dead because of sin and yet made alive by the Spirit. We are, therefore, called to walk in newness of life. Even though we have not experienced the final resurrection, we are called to live as a new creation. By living as new creatures, we are participating in the great reversal of sin. When we put to death the slavery of sin, we put on the new self, remade in the image of our Creator (Col. 3:8).

This is the life we ought to be calling our students to—a life of holiness.

The call to a lifestyle of holiness is nothing new. In fact, we find it as early as the second book of the Bible in the story of the Exodus. With great power and authority, God delivered Israel from the hands of the Egyptians and took them into the wilderness. Here God taught Israel how she would live with foreign nations on all sides. Israel was to be a people set apart for God. They were called to be a nation of priests, giving the surrounding nations a glimpse of the character and nature of the God of all creation. Despite their constant complaining and God's consequent provision, God's chosen nation made it to their destination. But the journey did not end there.

Throughout the Old Testament, the promise of resurrection encompasses the idea of a new creation, rescue from exile, and a new beginning. It is through the prophets we see the new creation coming, but it is the crucifixion and resurrection of Jesus which transforms the story of Israel from what could have been a tragic drama with little or no hope left and instead reaffirms Israel's hope into a beautifully orchestrated victory of God over the consequence of sin. The resurrection is the decisive event which demonstrates how God's kingdom really has been launched on earth as it is in heaven. Therefore, resurrection becomes a crucial and foundational belief for the disciple.

The resurrection begins the inauguration of:
    the new creation,
    the new Israel,
    the new promise,
    the new self,
    the new life,
    the pursuit of holiness,
    all of which are only possible through the resurrection of Jesus.

This image is beautifully captured by the prophet Ezekiel. A valley, dry and desolate—overtaken with death, the Lord commands the prophet to speak into the bones and God will breathe life into them (Ezek. 37:1–6). Piece by piece, what was once dead was coming back to life. The prophecy was intended for Israel; when all hope was lost, when they seem completely cut off from the divine breath, God would put His Spirit back in them and bring new life. But this prophecy also has significance for us. That same breath intended for Israel, to give her life, is also given to us through the Holy Spirit. It's the divine breath that gives us new life now so that we might live for His glory and purpose for our lives.

Before Christ, our old self is nothing more than dry bones rotting in the ground. It is not until the Spirit of God makes us into a new creation, breathes life into us, and invites us to live as truly human, made in the image of God (Rom. 8:9–11). Being in Jesus means that the mind is set on the Spirit, not the flesh; life, not death; grace, not the law. Pursuing holiness means that you live in tension between what once was and what will be.

Making It Stick

The nature of sin and the biblical solution to its infestation might seem, to older generations, to be entirely obvious and unnecessary to point out as a key part of being a disciple. However, when we consider the world our students are facing—one of rapidly deteriorating morality—its need is greater than ever. As youth leaders, we need to be able to move students from simply loving the idea of Jesus to deeply understanding their need for Him and the value of living the life He calls them to. Unfortunately, we have somehow allowed students to believe that forgiveness is the beginning and end of repentance and that what the Bible calls sin has to be weighed for its cultural relevancy. If our intention for them is nothing more than staying out of trouble, being a good person, and finding their true identity, then what room is left for Jesus?

So what's the plan? It's simple.

Talk about sin. Because we don't. Over the last ten years, I have lived in Detroit, Los Angeles, Chicago, and Fort Wayne, and of course attended different churches. In those ten years, I can count on one hand the number of times any one of those churches talked about sin. Why? Because it's easier to talk about how much Jesus loves us and the life He wants for us. It's more attractive to focus on the good in people, rather than the bad. But here's the thing: we aren't good. We are dirty, filthy sinners. A former colleague of mine used to tell his students that they were both divine and disgusting. He was insistent that they understood the nature of their flesh and the spiritual battle they were in every day.

Let's imagine for a moment what our students might be like if we never talked about the presence of sin. Now, I'm not talking about understanding the difference between right and wrong. God has already placed in us the inherent ability to recognize that there is a difference between the two. I'm talking about the explicit understanding of the Fall, depravity, and life in the flesh. They wouldn't have the ability to comprehend their moral inability to obey God, their inclination to self-justify, self-worship, and their natural bent toward choosing sin. Meaning for this group it would be impossible to pursue a holy lifestyle and life of discipleship; it would be impossible to please God and follow Him into the life He desires. Because such a life would be invisible, unknowable, and unreachable.

Recognizing the lordship of Jesus and the desire to be holy means first to recognize one's need for Jesus in the first place. If our students can't properly recognize the presence of sin in the world and in their lives, then what need do they have for Jesus? How could they possibly call Him Lord? Sin that we refuse to recognize poisons our hearts, hinders our worship, and our ability to impact the world with the gospel. How can we proclaim a gospel that we really don't fully accept because we don't fully accept our sin?

But we can't ignore the incredible challenge we face in our sin-erased, "This Is Me" culture. Many students and even some parents won't like it. You will no doubt hear comments like talking about sin is too negative, not loving enough, that kids won't respond, and so forth. But for anyone who is discipling youth, your job is to preach the gospel and live out its truth as an example. This includes sin. Without it, why are we even talking about the gospel, or even discipleship?

Living the life of a disciple is about a life in pursuit of holiness. Holiness requires the conquering of sin.
If we have any hope students will conquer sin, we need to talk about it.

It's true, our students are divine—as my colleague would put it. They are incredible kids, created in the image of God, special, purposed, and capable of more than we could possibly imagine. But they are truly disgusting. They are full of sin, destined in so many ways to choose evil over good, self over others, and their way over God's way. As leaders, we will watch, time and again, our students make decisions to willingly sin, justify it, excuse it, dismiss it, repent of it, and to our dismay, do it all over again.

However, contrary to mainstream and social media, I find that students deeply appreciate when adults stand firm on truth expressed in love toward those we disagree with or issues of sin. Culture may define tolerance as equal acceptance and validity of every individual and that no belief or behavior ought to be criticized, but true tolerance—the kind expressed by Christ Himself—is building relationships with people we disagree with. True tolerance is finding common ground without compromising convictions and allowing God's Word to guide how we understand what is true.

Practice it. Master it. It will pay great dividends as you connect with your students. But doing so requires that you are the first to model it. Remember, Paul told the Philippians to model the pattern he gave them (Phil. 2:17); the writer of Hebrews gave us numerous examples to follow (Heb. 11); Timothy was taught to serve as an example (1 Tim. 4:12–16), to name just a few. Students need to see how a life of holiness is realized in everyday situations. How they see you respond daily to life experiences and how you use the model given to us in Scripture. Living out the hope of Christ is a skill to be practiced and mastered—and, therefore, a skill to be taught.

God's commands for His people are not just a list of rules to follow, but the means of how to be the people He truly designed us to be. The law we discover in the Old Testament was given so that people would be aware of their sin and their need for Christ. But Jesus did not abolish the Law, suddenly giving us the freedom to act in any ridiculous way we choose. He fulfilled it. Giving us, through the Spirit, the means of living out God's purpose and ability to conquer sin and its effects. Read the Bible from the beginning, and it won't take very long to see how ugly sin makes things and the consequences of man's ideas versus the blessings of God's. Jesus' call to live a holy life is couched in the story of redemption and His own life, death, and resurrection. Jesus repeatedly showed His disciples life's important consequences by bringing them into situations where they could minister to the poor, the sick, and the grieving, raising their level of awareness of spiritual, physical, and emotional needs.[8]

Conclusion

Eliminating the old self and keeping in step with the Spirit allows disciples to experience the power of the resurrection and a life of holiness. Once our students begin to recognize sin and live according to the new self, ridding themselves of the old habits and practicing the new habits, they will experience the new life. The things once highly valued, the life that was intended to bring happiness and purpose, slowly loses significance, and the kingdom of God begins to take center stage. Life becomes focused on the mission to build the kingdom. The more focused disciples are on building the kingdom, the more intentional the pursuit of holiness and completion becomes—the closer students come to holiness and the closer they come to *telos*. To facilitate this movement, we must help them see the telos that shapes their actions, the virtues that support these larger ends, and the divine and human resources that exist too for them for a flourishing and virtuous Christian life.

6

SEEING PEOPLE
DIFFERENTLY

As the Father has sent me, so I am sending you.
Jesus (John 20:21)

I imagine that many of you have heard the quote that has been attributed to St. Francis of Assisi: "Preach the gospel at all times, and when necessary, use words." To be clear, chances are he never said that, and although I appreciate the sentiment, it is also not entirely accurate or biblical. The gospel requires both word and deed. But what I see more and more in our churches is the attitude of "preach the gospel at all times, so long as you're invited to share and won't offend anyone." But let's not immediately blame our young Christians for their reluctance and fear. As we have seen, our youth are faced with greater challenges to their faith than any previous generation in recent memory. Christian students are desperately trying to reconcile a radical faith in Christ with a culture actively rejecting Him.

Students want others to see them as loving and championing the causes of social justice. But if they disagree with others and that disagreement causes the other person some mental or social distress, the natural conclusion is that Christians must be unloving—or worse, hateful. The only alternative is to keep ourselves safe from those we disagree with. To avoid being the offender, we must agree or suppress our beliefs and opinions.

This is exactly where—and why—we have the creation of safe spaces, the avoidance of intellectual challenges and debate, and microaggressions. It is the dominance in the academic community of the ideological patterns of relativism—that every idea carries equal weight. Of course, only to exclude any idea that runs contrary. Speaking out against the majority groupthink unnecessarily discriminates and will likely cause such intense emotional harm to others that it is interpreted as an act of violence. In many parts of academia and the workplace, the Christian worldview and those who ascribe to it are seen as the enemy—if not personally, at least ideologically.

Who Gets the Moral High Ground?

Would you believe me if I told you nearly half of all Christians in their late twenties to late thirties consider it wrong to share their faith in Jesus with a person of a different faith or system of belief? And strikingly, more than half of that same age group rarely ever talk about their faith? Yeah, you read that right. According to a recent study done by Barna and Alpha USA, Millennial Christians may profess faith in Jesus but certainly have little to no interest in sharing it, and this is a part of a growing erosion in the Western church.

These are twenty- and thirty-something professionals who were some of the first to become regular users of modern technology, smartphones, and a world that is continuously connected. Millennials are also the pioneers of the social justice warriors on social media and many of the entrepreneurs of socially responsible companies. But during their time in college, we began to see a slow but steady deterioration of healthy academic debate, post-truth ideology, relativism, and an ever-shifting morality. Loving others means affirming previously immoral lifestyles. Speaking out against a more progressive ideology is now the equivalent to spreading hate speech against a minority group.

I recently met a young youth pastor, just beginning in his ministry. He was lamenting that he didn't have many students and couldn't seem to find the right "event formula" to attract them. So I asked him how many times he had been to the local high schools. His response: "None." I asked how many teachers and administrators he knew. "None." I asked how many times he had visited during events like See You at the Pole and National Day of Prayer. "None." I even asked if he tried to connect with the school's sports teams to offer volunteer help. Not a single one. So naturally, I wondered why. Not only did it never occur to him, but once I offered the suggestions, he balked at the idea of bringing Jesus to the public square. The same is true of many young parents I know. Sharing one's faith is just simply not part of the equation. A private and sacred faith has no place in a highly secularized culture. And with each passing generation, the number who believe this is growing. So on the one hand, GenZ kids are being taught to privatize their faith and keep it to themselves, and on the other hand, they are trying to live a Christian life in a post-Christian culture.

The moral high ground belongs to the culturally tolerant. Keeping one's faith private and staying in step with mainstream culture, no matter how contrary it may run to one's belief system, is what it means to love others, embrace humanity, and live a morally upright life.

Think of it this way—proclaiming the gospel, confronting people with their sins, even verbalizing that Jesus is the only means of salvation will most likely be seen as hateful and an act of emotional violence on another person or group. Loving another person in our modern Western culture no longer means throwing them a lifeline to save them from a destructive life of sin and an eternity without God. Instead, it implies affirmation and celebration of any lifestyle one chooses. The moral high ground now belongs to the one who lives and let lives, puts feelings before facts, and places all worldviews on equal footing. As David Kinnaman noted in a recent Barna study, "Cultivating deep, steady, resilient Christian conviction is difficult in a world of 'you do you' and 'don't criticize anyone's life choices' and emotivism, the feelings-first priority that our culture makes as a way of life."[1]

So how we understand the mission given to the church and how we help our students walk that journey is vital to the life of the church.

Defining the Mission

When I look at the earliest days of the church, I see the same fear, the same reluctance, and in fact, many of the same cultural challenges. Remember, the Jews crucified Jesus because He posed a threat—religiously, socially, and politically. His claim to be God in the flesh radically challenged their worldview in a way the Jewish elite simply could not handle. Jesus' death didn't immediately eliminate the threat. So naturally, rumors of His resurrection made things so much worse.

Post-resurrection, the disciples locked themselves in a room, because they were afraid (John 20:19). Perhaps afraid they too would be crucified, afraid because Jesus' tomb was empty and dead people don't usually wake up, and maybe afraid for what would happen next. After all, they had just spent three years with Jesus, so it's likely they had some idea that news of Jesus' appearance meant God was up to something.

Amid that fear, Jesus appeared and reminded them of their mission, "Just as the Father has sent me, so I am sending you" (John 20:19). God wants to send out His people to be His representatives, conduits of His love, and make His kingdom known. Between this moment, the Great Commission (Matthew 28), and the moments just before Jesus' ascension (Acts 1:8), we see very clearly God's intention for the church. In fact, that has been God's intention for humanity all along.

Since sin entered the world, God has employed His people to live on mission to reunite humanity with Him. The Exodus, Mount Sinai, the Law, the Promised Land, the return from exile, Jesus, and now the church, have all been part of a grand narrative of God working through His people to rescue the world. Israel was called to be a holy nation and a kingdom of priests. From Genesis through Revelation, God did not call His people just to do certain things or obey specific laws, but to be a certain kind of people. On that riverbank, on the brink of the Promised Land, God's chosen people had not finished their journey. The Jordan River was not the means to an end. Israel was blessed with the Promised Land in order to be a blessing to the surrounding nations. They were to be a city on a hill, a light in the middle of the darkest places. The same holds true for the church and every single one of our students.

The church is called to *be* salt and light, to *go* and make disciples, and to *speak* truth in love. It is the all-encompassing purpose of humanity.

So the mission is to be like Jesus. Which is precisely what the disciples did. After Jesus launched them into ministry, Peter and John came across a crippled man at the steps of the Temple in Jerusalem (Acts 3:1–10). The man was placed in front of the Temple each day so he could beg from people as they made their way in to worship. This man, from birth, could not walk. He was cast out from the rest of society and dependent upon everyone else to survive. He was a slave to his condition, crying out for deliverance.

Think about this for a moment, though. Our power to be mobile, our strength to stand, comes from our legs. Our ankles and feet provide the stability to walk. There is a certain sense of freedom given. Certainly, now, technology has advanced us in so many ways, and many people are no longer hindered by such a setback. But think of the first century. Without the power of your legs, opportunities were quite limited, at least in the Jewish mind-set. One would spend a lifetime seeking compassion from others, desperately trying to maintain the hope for freedom.

Jesus' ministry on earth was filled with the healing of the lame, sick, blind, even dead—many of which were considered the least of society, slaves to their condition, crying out for deliverance from their circumstances. They needed compassion. Each of these healing moments pointed to Jesus and the restoration and the freedom He would bring. Each of these moments pointed to a God who was rescuing His people. When John the Baptist looked for assurance that Jesus was the Messiah, Jesus replied, "Go back and report to John what you hear and see: The blind receive sight, the lame walk, those who have leprosy are cleansed, the deaf hear, the dead are raised, and the good news is proclaimed to the poor" (Matt.11:4–5). Those were the clear signs that God had indeed arrived, the kingdom had come, and rescue was in progress.

Peter and John, however, broke from the norm and recognized a greater need and an even greater opportunity. There was certainly compassion, just not at all what the lame man thought. No money in hand, Peter and John gave him the only thing they could. With just a few words, Peter took the man by the hand and immediately the man's feet and ankles became strong (Acts 3:6–7). Despite his affliction, this man believed in the name of Jesus, the credibility, the promises, the very nature of who Jesus is. This man believed in the mission of God.

But Peter and John did not stop at the healing. They used this as an opportunity to connect the name and power of Jesus the Messiah with the God of Abraham, Isaac, and Jacob. The onlookers were Jewish, and they knew the story of the Exodus; they remembered the cry of their ancestors enslaved in Egypt. Peter and John made it absolutely clear that repentance and faith through Jesus are the only means by which God would finally deliver His people.

The paradigm of God's redemptive nature had taken a dramatic shift. According to Jewish tradition, all they were required to do was throw some money at this man and move on. That was compassion enough. But instead of being comfortable with the status quo, they heard the cry of the oppressed lame man, and they followed the example of Jesus and went above and beyond. They understood that recognizing Jesus as Messiah meant recognizing His role concerning God's mission for Israel for the blessing of all nations. They found themselves determined to break tradition and go above and beyond what was required.

This is precisely what Jesus meant when He spoke of the coming kingdom. Jesus brought with Him the model of the kingdom, freedom, rest, restoration, and finally, resurrection. When Jesus returned to the Father, the disciples began to carry out the mission that Jesus had begun. The mission that now belongs to the church.

See People Differently

Are we really asking students to live on mission by walking up to perfect strangers and trying to heal them? Perhaps that could happen. I know a handful of students that have traveled oversees on various mission trips and have experienced similar events of healing—and it changed them forever. But that's not the lesson this passage is teaching. First, Peter and John *saw* this man. They didn't just give money and move on. They didn't just fulfill their religious obligations; they were salt and light by doing exactly what Jesus would have done—they had compassion on this man. Second, not only did they speak truth to the lame man, they used the opportunity to speak truth to everyone watching, and again later when questioned by Jewish authorities.

This man's needs went beyond physical affliction. Peter and John met the man's spiritual need. The healing, enabled by the Spirit, provided the platform to proclaim the name of Jesus. This is the lesson for our students. Our students have a greater capacity to reach the lost than most adults. Nearly every day, they are surrounded by opposing and often antagonistic worldviews. They are swimming in a sea of lost people. There is no greater mission field in Western culture than in the context of our students.

The mission for our students is not just a matter of a simple declaration that Jesus is Lord, nor is it simply a matter of speaking about it. The centrality of the mission of God mimics the actions of Peter and John on the steps of the Temple. There are countless people in our neighborhoods and communities who are crying out for deliverance because of some kind of enslavement. In every grocery store, coffee shop, school, workplace, family cookout, and shopping mall, there are people in pain and in need of rescue. This is the mission God has given His people and sets the stage for what is on the other side of the river and what life will look like once we are across.

Disciples are called to live it. We are called to be a part of the mission, be a part of compassion, be a part of the restoration of the broken. We are called to live as the people God created us to be. We are called to live the mission of the kingdom of God, with Jesus as Lord, from heaven to earth.

The Reality for Our Students

Sounds great, doesn't it? Yes, culture is difficult, but we have Jesus in our corner. We are empowered by the Spirit. So even if living out God's mission is hard, our students should feel confident no matter the cost. Right?

I wish it were that easy. Anytime I have a chance to talk with students, I ask them what it's like to share their faith. The topic of sharing their faith is a severe point of stress for them—what Jesus demands of them versus what they feel culture allows. To help me understand where this stress comes from, I typically get five recurring and specific points from the students.

What Will People Think of Me?

Despite what we believe or wish to be the case, social pressure among our students is real. And I'm not talking about the influence of negative peer pressure that most adults dealt with as children. Social media platforms have taken social pressure to an entirely new level. Share Jesus or show your Christian self to the wrong person, and you could drastically jeopardize social standing, friendships, and even opportunities within the school. Browse through Twitter for a second, and you'll see the constant barrage of hate.

But as the adult leader, you are likely thinking that our students ought to willingly endure persecution, ridicule, and scorn for the joy of sharing one's faith. But if we are honest with ourselves, we know that is a lot easier said than done. This obstacle is hard enough for an adult to overcome. Imagine how difficult it is for our students. Especially in a culture increasingly hostile toward Christians.

Turning People Off to Christ

This is purely a confidence issue. And rightly so. It is a question of preparedness, and it compels us to ask ourselves as pastors and leaders of youth: Are we thoroughly training them? I know we can't give them all the answers, but trust me; they are not fretting over deep theological questions that trip up even the best seminary grads. I am talking about the simplicity of sharing the gospel, a more in-depth and proper understanding of salvation. And most importantly, how on earth do they confront the sins of their time when much of it is not considered sin?

Many students express a sincere desire to represent Christ well, and they don't want to be the cause of someone turning from Christ or worse, causing someone to come to Him under false pretenses or misunderstanding.

Not Really Knowing the Baggage People Are Carrying

Anxiety, depression, social pressures, academic performance, broken families, gender identity, and dysphoria, and way too much screen time. All of these and so much more are adding countless pounds to the amount of baggage our students are dealing with day in and day out. But in just a few brief conversations with students, I learned of the incredible sensitivity to each other's life issues one is dealing with at any given moment. They understand that every problem is highly individualized and unique to each student. Rather than make assumptions, they appreciate the need to peel back the layers before rushing into a Jesus conversation.

Automatic Judgment

Imagine approaching someone you know. Maybe a neighbor, co-worker, or family member. You intend to look for an opening for a great Jesus conversation. You're not trying to save them right this instant, but you want to see if they are at least open to the idea of Jesus. But the minute they even smell a little bit of Jesus on you, they immediately label you as homophobic, bigoted, hateful, and even racist. Even your best intentions are widely misconstrued as an act of violence directed at them.

Perhaps this sounds crazy, but this is the reality on many college campuses and is quickly trickling down to local high schools. The value of honest, intellectual, and respectful debate is becoming a thing of the past. Permission to disagree and offer alternative opinions does not come from debates and arguments, it comes from relationships.

Relational Development

Take a step back and look deeper into the issue and you quickly notice that so much of this boils down to relationships. Almost intuitively, students understand the great power behind building relationships with others and the power it has when we look for open doors for the gospel. Their desire for deeper relationships helps us see the importance of how others see them, judge them, and the baggage others are carrying. This rising generation of students has dialed into something we can all benefit from—relationships. Not just a means to introduce people to Jesus, but a necessary foundation for building community and making disciples.

Spend any time talking with students about sharing their faith, and you will no doubt discover they have a sincere desire to help their friends, classmates, and teammates meet Jesus and experience salvation. However, you may also find that we, as leaders, make far too many assumptions. No doubt living out our faith in the public square and sharing the love of Jesus with words and actions is an essential part of what it means to follow Jesus. But I also think we need to appreciate how difficult that can be for the rising generation. Certainly not as an excuse to hide, but so that we can walk alongside them, build confidence in them, support and mentor them.

GETTING LOVE RIGHT

*Do not waste time bothering whether
you love your neighbor; act as if you did.*

C.S. Lewis

One of the most difficult parts of the Christian walk for our students is trying to figure out how in the world do they express love—the Jesus kind—yet stick to truth? As leaders we tell them all the time to "love their neighbor," yet forget to realize that loving their neighbor in their highly digitized, post-truth, post-Christian, morally relative, safe-space driven, call-out culture is far different than expressing love in the world you and I grew up in. Ask your students what the second greatest commandment looks like if you haven't already. While the answers do vary a bit, the general consensus of answers largely attempts to love people as they are. In fact, most of our students are the poster children for tolerance—as far as culture sees it.

As I have mentioned, our youth have been indoctrinated with the idea that true love is the unconditional acceptance and endorsement of any behavior a person chooses to engage in. Loving others means being keenly aware of others' triggers and complete unfettered adherence to the rules of cultural tolerance: "what every individual believes or says is equally right and equally valid, and that no individual's belief or behavior should be judged or criticized."[1] In other words, to love is not only acceptance, but affirmation of another's lifestyle. And for the Christian student, that means affirmation regardless of the sin. To make this idea a little easier to swallow in our Christian circles, we often identify this as grace.

They Have It All Wrong

In my original outline of this book, I didn't include a chapter on love. I figured it was a no-brainer. But the more conversations I had with students and parents, the more I noticed the desire to love wasn't an issue. I was right about that. But what I got wrong was how that love is manifested in the daily lives of believers—especially our youth. Generation Z might be the most loving generation in recent history. But they have little idea of what love actually looks like. My goal in this chapter is not to tell you that Christians ought to love—I think you know that—but to explore what your students believe love is, what our culture teaches compared to Jesus' teaching, and how to help our students see the difference.

During my few short years as a high school football coach, I had incredible opportunities to challenge and mentor my young players. But every once in a while, that process locked horns with parents. Jerry and Nick were two of my star players. Their natural talent and importance to the team's chances of winning made it easy to forgive and forget minor transgressions in school, on the field, or even at home. Just a few weeks into the season, heading into a rival game, I caught wind that Jerry and Nick were caught smoking on school grounds. A clear violation of school policy and team rules.

That would make Friday night's game much more of a challenge. But I felt I had little choice. I had to suspend them. Nothing huge, but they would sit on the bench and watch this week. By the time the school day came to an end, I was met with cries from their parents to have grace. From their perspective, I had an opportunity to take my goal of mentoring to a whole new level, show them love by showing them grace; show them the love of God by letting them play. These parents were asking me to be culturally tolerant by turning a blind eye to their sin—and call it love.

But that's only one side of this complex love issue. For as many parents and students I had calling for extreme levels of grace—which actually translated into a misunderstanding of grace—I had equally as many crying for more rules and restrictions and yet still calling it love. Should we let students dance at events like homecoming and prom? How long (or short) should girls' skirts be? How long should boys' hair be? And can they wear earrings? What about tattoos? Now some of you reading this have very specific and detailed opinions about each of these questions. All of which likely come from a place of love for students.

How easy—and often necessary—is it to raise and mentor our kids by equating good behavior with avoiding bad behavior? As every parent of young children knows, the list of what to avoid seems endless. Children have to be told *not* to play on the stairs, *not* to run with scissors, and *not* to climb up a slide backwards. These instructions create habits of parenting and mentoring that translate into similar lists of what not to do when attempting to teach obedience and discipleship. But following Jesus is not adherence to a laundry list of benchmarks one needs to hit in order to make the team; rather, it's learning what it means to live out the second greatest commandment, "love your neighbor as yourself" (Matt. 22:39).

We believe if they don't look like the world, there is less chance they'll act like it. And to some degree that is true. But your students often see that expression of love as oppressive, unforgiving, restrictive, and irrelevant—rules designed to make life miserable. Although our intentions come from the desire to speak truth at all costs, too often that expression of truth is seen as counterproductive, intolerant, and perhaps hateful. I saw this kind of thing emerge in students like Kim.

Kim was raised in a strict Christian home with several siblings and loving parents. She was raised to be loving, but felt her parents' restrictions and rules had no place in a faith filled with grace. Her response to her family life, which might seem on the surface to be the more loving option, actually began to reject the teachings of Jesus altogether. Anytime I mentioned the moral obligations of

Scripture or discussed Jesus as the only means of salvation (John 14:6), she would get angry and argue that my position was unloving. At the same time using the same author, John, to further her own point—that God is love (1 John 4:8). The problem was that Kim was wrestling with wanting to love Jesus, obey her parents, and follow the rules—including the rules of cultural tolerance.

Kim's view, and that of many like her, has created a wild misunderstanding of what it truly means to love God and love our neighbors. And perhaps responses like Kim's have caused the adults in her life to dig their heels in deeper, creating more rules and obligations, driving a deeper wedge between generations—making it that much more difficult to make disciples of our students.

If we don't get love right, then the rest of the chapters in this book are quite meaningless.

The Best Kind of Neighbor

When we think of love in the Christian sense of the word, we likely think of the Greek word *agape*. It's the kind of love that is action-oriented and sacrificial, and it serves as the most accurate description of God's love for us and His commandment to love our neighbors. But that's where we stop. That's the end of our lesson for students. We stress the idea that real love can't just endorse any and every kind of behavior—even if it's destructive. We are also sure to mention that it's no more loving to condemn people living a lifestyle that contradicts biblical teaching. *Agape* is seeking the best interest of another. It means putting others before ourselves. It's a hard feeling to describe, but we often know it when we see it. For me, it was that moment when I watched my bride make her way down the aisle, the first time I held my oldest daughter, Hannah, and the few days I had to watch my second oldest, Leah, suffer with an allergic reaction I couldn't do anything about. In those kinds of moments, putting another person first isn't a thought, it's action. It's a reflex.

But as beautiful as this kind of love is, it still falls short of God's intention if we fail to teach our students the difference between culturally tolerant love and biblically accurate love. Yes, love is still about putting others first, but what does that look like?

The love which God extends to us is expressed best through hope. Because of Jesus we have hope. We have a second chance. Despite so much going wrong in the garden, God provided a means of hope—because He loves us. Even when Israel felt all hope was lost, God sent His son to live the life we couldn't and to be the sacrifice we should have been and enacted the resurrection to prove it. Jesus was hope incarnate. Hope is about setting things back the way they are supposed to be—a global scale restoration. In our redemption and our own personal restoration, we have been given that hope. The love we set out to show others, our act of putting others first, is passing that hope on—paying it forward. This is the kind of love that fulfills loving one's neighbor.

We know this because Jesus modeled it for us.

The Sabbath, Hope, and Love

Like any normal Saturday, Jesus made His way to the synagogue. But this time, Jesus made a decision to heal a guy with a deformed hand. Knowing the Jewish religious leadership was looking for a reason to get rid of Him, Jesus called this guy to the front, and before healing him, asked an interesting question. He said in Mark 3:4, "Which is lawful on the Sabbath: to do good or to do evil, to save life or to kill?"

Now remember on the Sabbath a Jew wasn't allowed to work. Rabbis spent many hours deliberating what actually constituted work, and healing in this case was unanimously voted as work, therefore a violation of the Mosaic Law and which, of course, helped them build their case against Jesus. But Jesus healed the man anyway.

You probably have the same questions I do. First, what's the big deal about healing on the Sabbath; after all, how much "work" was that miracle for Jesus? Second, Jesus would have known healing this guy was going to stir up controversy, so why take the risk? Finally, why did Jesus talk about saving a life or killing? The man had a deformity; he wasn't dying. If he was, Old Testament law would have allowed saving his life on the Sabbath. The work it would take to save a life is excused under the law.

Jesus' decision to heal this man was motivated by more than just making the Pharisees crazy (although I'm convinced that's part of it). Jesus was actually demonstrating the kind of love God desires versus what the Pharisees thought it was. We often accuse the Pharisees of legalism, but really what they were doing was performing what was considered cultural tolerance in the first century. Much like our friend Kim. She said she loved God, but her love for others was distorted and misguided by the influence of cultural tolerance. The religious leaders of Jesus' day suffered from a similar influence, but by creating rules they, boosted their own self-righteousness and suppressed hope rather than providing it. They would have rather let this man suffer one more day—calling it obedience, than showing love toward this man by demonstrating the hope-filled, restorative purpose of the Sabbath.

The Sabbath is about rest and reliance on God's provision and promises. Essentially, the Sabbath is about hope. It points us back to Him and our reliance on His provision for our lives. Essentially, the future is in His hands. Jesus showed perfect love toward this man, not just by healing him, but doing so on the Sabbath, giving us a picture of God's restoration, the very foundation in which our hope is built; "for God so loved the world, that He gave His one and only son" (John 3:16). Jesus heals this man to give us a glimpse of restoration in action, hope breaking through, and the love of God ignited in another person.

Love does not condemn, it gives hope. Love sends the woman at the well back into town filled with hope (John 4:39–42). Love compelled the accusers of the adulterous woman to drop their stones leaving her to live another day filled with hope (John 8:11).

Love was every time Jesus chose to connect with and eat with tax collectors and sinners, sending a message of hope. And love was the day Jesus handed Himself over to be crucified, fulfilling hope for the entire world.

This is the kind of love we want to see in our students. The goal for every disciple is to be like Jesus, meaning we need to love like Him by ushering hope into another person's world—meeting Jesus through us. Every time we succumb to the belief that love is defined by cultural tolerance, we are stripping people of all hope. Every time we believe people have a right to behave in any way they choose—endorsing and approving it—we are denying them the freedom of living the life God designed.

Making It Stick

You may have noticed that most of our youth—if not all—already know they should love others. In fact, that is one of the great things about GenZ. They have a great capacity to love others. Largely because they see people differently—better in fact. They live in a more diverse world and love it. Being so connected to the rest of the world has opened their eyes to injustice and they want desperately to right the wrongs of the world. They love the idea of being conduits of hope in the lives of others. But here's the thing. As youth leaders, we have to help them experience what it means to reflect the love of Christ—through experience; it's how they are wired to learn. It is what is necessary if our students are going to thrive on the opposite banks of the river. You don't need a new program or some complex system; you just need a few simple steps. Let me show you what I mean.

Pray

Zac's dad was your typical tough guy. Never once did Zac see his dad cry, be really sad, or even really happy. Until one night, Zac had woken up only a few hours after going to bed. Needing a drink of water, he headed down the stairs to the kitchen. What he discovered would change his relationship with his father forever; and to be honest, change the trajectory of his life.

His dad was praying. Not for himself. He wasn't trying to wrestle through a tough situation at work or in marriage. He was praying for everyone he knew who didn't know Jesus. But that's not the best part. As this man prayed, he wept. He was literally crying out to God asking for help to reach his friends who did not yet know Jesus.

Before that moment, Zac's exposure to prayer was limited to a few times in church, prayers before dinner and bed, and the occasional personal plea for help in a difficult situation. But in that moment, Zac saw prayer impact the posture of his father's heart towards others.

Jesus taught us that we should pray for our enemies and those who persecute us. We should pray for the salvation of others, pray that we don't fall into temptation, and pray that God's will be done. Prayer is certainly the ongoing communication with God, but it also serves as the litmus test of the true condition of our hearts. We have to get our students to move beyond the routine prayers before meals and bed, get beyond praying before taking a test, having a personal problem, or reserving it for Sundays. When we teach our students to practice the spiritual habit of prayer—for others—it will fundamentally change how they see those people, how they talk to them, and how they treat them.

If we are teaching our students to love like Jesus, it has to begin with prayer.

Seek Intentionally

Narcissism is on the rise. Self-promotion is an art form on social media, and given the number of safe spaces, trigger warnings, and cries of victimhood on college campuses around the United States, it's easy to see just who our students are being taught to care about the most—themselves.

Instead of being offended at nearly everything, we can teach students to intentionally seek the good for others. When I propose this idea of intentionally seeking out others, most pastors and parents jump to getting students involved in serving their community. And that is a good first step. But I want to challenge you to go bigger. Let's be honest; for most of us, serving total strangers—while helpful, needed, and used to grow us spiritually—can take us only so far. They are strangers. We likely won't ever see them again. Challenge your students to serve their friends, teachers, coaches, and family members—people they will see frequently.

But how? First, start with conversations. Don't assume your students know how to effectively communicate with another person. But teaching them how to listen, how to ask great questions, and how to express empathy will have profound impact on their relationships.

Second, help students see what serving others as a daily habit looks like. Teaching students Christ-like love has to get beyond the biannual service project. For serving to be an extension and expression of love for our neighbors, it has to become part of the rhythm of our daily routines. Maybe it's helping clean a classroom, helping a fellow student with homework, doing the dishes at home without being asked, or just listening to someone vent about their day. When we serve others without the interference of our narcissistic tendencies, we can forever change the course of that relationship. Thereby opening the doors for truth-driven, gospel-saturated conversations.

The goal is to enter into a deeper conversation in order to build a relationship that offers hope. That kind of depth doesn't happen by silently pouring soup into the bowl of a homeless person.

Share Truth Boldly

This can be where trying to love like Christ can get tricky. For many of us—students included—the minute we start talking about sharing truth, we become filled with fear and anxiety. But unless we confront and address the dangers of cultural tolerance and look out for the best interests of others, we aren't being loving. Christlike love is the kind of love that infuses darkness with light and exposes destructive behaviors in others. I love how Sean and Josh McDowell put it: "Truth is our best friend, and it is an inseparable part of what real love is. While cultural tolerance may disguise itself as caring, understanding, and loving, it lacks the moral authority of an authentic love that looks out for the best interest of others."[2] If love is going to be others-focused, then we must be able to speak truth boldly.

This doesn't mean pointing out every flaw, sin, or questionable behavior to everyone we meet. Unless of course you're looking for the fastest way to be seen as a hypocrite and a self-righteous jerk. I'm guessing that as a youth leader you're not aiming to make disciples who people hate. But that's where the fear settles in. We believe that sharing truth will actually make us appear to be unloving. The trick is learning to ask good, thought-provoking questions rather than simply making assertions. Telling someone they are wrong sounds mean and hurtful. Asking someone why they think they're right creates deeper conversations and builds trust. Shoving Jesus down a person's throat is often too forceful for people to accept. But offering Jesus as the true source of hope shows them you might actually care.

As youth leaders we need to remind students it's never their job to save anyone. That's God's job, and we ought to be glad to let Him do it. Our job is to love others. Pray for them. Seek them out and serve them. And share the truth of Jesus with them. Leave the rest up to the Spirit of God. We are simply joining in a conversation God is already having with that person. If our students are truly working to love others, people will begin to see them less and see Jesus more.

8

THE POWER OF THE TRIBE

We cannot live only for ourselves.
A thousand fibers connect us with our fellow men.

Herman Melville

If I leave for work in the morning at just the right time, it will take me nearly ten to twenty extra minutes to just leave the subdivision. Because chances are I am going to get stuck behind a school bus. Any other time during the day you'd never know it, but our neighborhood has an incredibly dense population of elementary and middle school kids. It seems like there is a bus stop on literally every corner—kids everywhere. But drive through on a sunny Saturday afternoon in the summer and there won't be a kid in sight. Instead, they sit inside starring at a screen. Most studies suggest that kids ages eight to eighteen spend nearly seven hours a day looking at a device. Screen time has officially replaced playtime.

But it's also replacing real face-to-face social interaction, which drastically impacts how our kids create community. Our students are longing for connection, but the traditional teen hangout activities like the malls, parties, driving around, or the literal act of doing "nothing" have been replaced by digital activities. Ask a student why they tend to ignore or even avoid in-person social interaction, they will tell you, "it's just easier."

Students spend less time outside, less time engaging in face-to-face interactions, and possess lesser degrees of social skills; instead, they spend more time online engaged in social media, gaming, or streaming services like Netflix. In fact, given the choice, many students would rather engage digitally in the comfort of their home rather than meeting up at the mall or hanging with friends. But our students did not create this world; they were born into it. Students were born into a world less connected to community, raised by parents who spend more time commuting to and from work and less time getting to know the neighbors—doors closed, curtains drawn, shutting out the rest of the world so we can view it through a screen.

It might be the only world our students know, but their own reality is causing more harm than good. Students may be more connected to the world, but they are also more stressed, more depressed, and have greater levels of anxiety. Suicide rates continue to rise as GenZ's overall reported happiness continues to decline.

The simple reality is we have the need to belong, be unified, and relevant. We want people to hear our opinions, like our statuses, the places we go, and the food we eat, but we want all of those things while hiding behind our firewalls. We live in a world that gives us the ability to reach more people at a much faster pace and yet we spend more time alone than a generation ago. If adults are guilty of this tendency just imagine what our students are dealing with. They have greater means of communication and capacity to reach people than any generation before them but have little idea how to communicate face-to-face. They have been given a way to avoid real social interaction.

But it's not God's design and it's not healthy for development of our students let alone discipleship. Dr. Jean Twenge's research of Generation Z shows the clear correlation between screen time and unhappiness and loneliness. In fact, the younger the student, the greater likelihood they will be affected by screen time. Twenge found out that "teens who visit social networking sites every day are actually more likely to agree 'I feel lonely,' 'I feel left out of things,' and 'I often wish I had more good friends.' In contrast, those who spend more time with their friends in person or who play sports are less lonely."[1] But none of us should be that surprised. The digital world only makes us appear to be more connected while creating a larger disconnect to the real world. The

God-intended benefits of community and social interaction can't be found anywhere in the digital landscape.

God designed us for community, and I believe we are begging for it—especially our students. But instead, our Western culture has fooled us into thinking that social media supplies us with the kind of community people are searching for. We need community, but instead we live in houses that are too big, farther away from neighbors, and have taller privacy fences. It's even seen in today's families, who are failing to live in community in their own house; eating meals at different times and in different parts of the house. We need community because, despite the false substitutes, we were never designed to be alone. From the beginning, God's design was relationship, intimacy, and community. When God created Adam and placed him in the garden to work and care for it, He knew the need for community (Gen. 2:18–23).

God's Design

Adam was created in the image of God, and yet was alone. If Adam was to truly reflect the image of God, then community was necessary. It is God Himself who reflects the perfect community. The coeternal, coexistent triune Godhead is the perfect model of community. God the Father, God the Son, and God the Holy Spirit exist and operate as one in perfect love and community. Living as one in spirit and mind, God exists as three personalities, at the same time equally one God. When we as people created in the image of God enter into relationships—entering into community, we become a more complete representation of God's image in man. Humanity's original purpose was to be fruitful and fill the earth and to reflect the very essence of God on earth. Being alone prevents man from fulfilling God's design. Consequently, isolation makes it impossible to carry out the mission.

The intention of community did not stop with Adam and Eve, but it continued with the covenant God made with Abraham—he would be the father of a great nation. God used one man to begin a community, working to restore the broken image of God in man. This was the very essence of Israel's mission. They were called as a community of people to live together as a people belonging to God, a priesthood displaying to the nations the God of all creation. They traveled through the desert as a community; they conquered other nations as a community; they rebuilt the walls of Jerusalem as a community. The nation of Israel was treated as one unified people, a community.

If we, as disciples of Jesus, are going to properly reflect the image of God as we were created to, we cannot continue to pretend that social media is community, texting friends is community, or spending evenings binge watching Netflix and YouTube are community. We cannot attend church like we attend the movies; showing up in time to grab a snack, enjoy the show, and go home. We cannot pretend that we can find satisfaction in Christ as some personal spiritual journey, traveled in solitude. Fulfillment in Jesus Christ cannot be found solely in the private contemplative life of religious piety. And we certainly cannot afford to pass this mentality on to our students.

Our brains are wired for tribalism. We are drawn to people groups who are like-minded and will go to great lengths to support and defend our tribe. This is precisely the way God set up the nation of Israel. One nation made up of many tribes—family groups of people who stuck together at all costs. When we feel connected to our tribe, it's like a switch is flipped, and we bind ourselves to our group, we embrace and defend the group's moral matrix, and we actually stop thinking for ourselves.[2] In fact some even find themselves blind to arguments and information that challenges the tribe's narrative.[3]

Tribes

My college days were spent at Michigan State University. During those years, my friends and I would frequently make the short sixty-mile trip southeast to Ann Arbor, the home of The University of Michigan—Michigan State's largest rival school. Although we considered ourselves brave and even a little dumb, we never went alone. Instead, we went with a large group on a big MSU bus, seeking to make a lot of noise and get a lot of attention. We often found ourselves being harassed by the Michigan faithful, but we continued our pursuit of ridiculous behavior in the name of college rivalry. We all knew if any one of us attempted such bravery on our own, we would have chickened out.

But because of the community my friends and I had as MSU Spartans, we developed what is known as minimal group paradigm—a methodology used in social psychology to measure discrimination among people groups using arbitrary criteria. In 1971 there was a social psychologist named Henri Tajfel, who was deeply and personally impacted by Nazi Germany in WW II. Tajfel wanted to figure out the conditions under which people would discriminate against people of a different group. Using a series of carefully devised experiments, he found "that no matter how trivial or 'minimal' he made the distinctions between their groups, people tended to distribute whatever was offered in favor of their in-group members."[4] Tajfel's study inspired others like it—all aimed at discovering how people in one group respond to others of another group.

So what happens when our students find their tribe early in middle or high school? They find their group, those they have common ground with, those they will defend, and those who craft our students' moral matrix. Have you ever wondered why it is so difficult to convince some students of such basic principles like a universal standard of morality? When our students are engaged in that tribal mode, their brain is literally shut off from opposing arguments. The gospel becomes offensive because it threatens that student's tribe.

The unfortunate reality is that our sports teams and political convictions foster stronger, bolder, and more unified communities than our churches do. My friends at Michigan State were my tribe. There were always people you did not know, people you didn't agree with, even people you did not like, but on Saturday afternoons we all bled green and white. Wearing blue and maize (The University of Michigan's colors) was grounds for social ostracism. Even today, almost twenty years later, when I step foot on campus, there is that same sense of community and tribalism. This same principle applies when trying to create community with our students. You're not just working to create community within the church; you're likely working against other tribes the students belong to. When we belong and we feel that what we do and think matters, even if only to a few, we become unified with those of like-mindedness. But what would it look like if our students found their tribe inside the church community? For an answer, we need to return to Peter and John in Acts chapter four.

The Power of Community

We introduced the story of Peter and John healing a lame man outside the Temple in chapter six. The healing of this man created not only a firestorm of controversy but a tremendous opportunity. It was an opportunity to present the gospel, the power of God in Christ, and a catalyst for boldness. Peter and John had every reason to run and hide—retreat and live to fight another day. The Jewish leadership warned them to stop talking about Jesus or there would be greater consequences than just temporary imprisonment and a stern warning. They could have been facing death. To the contrary, Peter and John purposefully stood out, risked everything, counted on being noticed, and looked forward to whatever consequences came their way (Acts 4:18–20). They were so compelled by the gospel, and so convinced of its truth, they could do nothing but speak of the things they had seen and heard (Acts 4:20).

When Peter and John were released from custody, they reported back to the community of believers what had taken place. Something began to happen. The boldness of Peter and John began to spread throughout the rest of the community of believers.

Their actions created an air of community among the believers—a great multitude joined in prayer, worship, meeting physical needs and suffering. They were united. They were committed to each other under the guidance of the Spirit and love for each other (Acts 4:23–31).

This community of early church believers broke all the barriers of what was considered the community of the people of God in the Jewish religious system. The community of Israel was once joined by law and ritual, joined by nationality and birth right, joined by the promise of a nation and land. The disciples of Jesus Christ were joined in authentic love for each other, joined by the need to carry out the mission of the gospel, joined by perseverance while they waited for the coming kingdom, making it a reality on earth in the meantime. They made community tangible and something to be sought after.

Their willingness had a cascading effect on the rest of the Christian community, solidifying their tribal mentality, unifying the church, and enabling them to proclaim the name of Jesus boldly. This community of believers was more than about what they had in common, where they lived, or even what they believed. This community was about the Spirit of God animating their entire being and what they desired. This is the power of community—of a tribe.

As we direct our students in becoming effective disciples, we cannot neglect the power communities can have over our students. We can't just spend large portions of our budgets on events and training for our students in one capacity or another, equipping them to share the gospel, somehow hoping it will translate into spiritual maturity and discipleship. Because, at the first sign of trouble, they're likely to sink back into their seats and try to just blend in—holding on to the satisfaction that they at least tried—doing something rather than just nothing. But when the learning is over and it's time to head back home—back to normality—the excitement will fizzle out, the boldness will fade away, the mountain-top experience is only a memory, and life needs to return to normal. It's the community, the tribe that has the capacity to rally together and reignite the passion to share and follow Jesus.

Every single youth leader questions why the magic is lost seconds after students leave an intense spiritual atmosphere and return to their school and family communities. It's the entire reason you wanted them trained in the first place—to go into their world for the sake of their world. What we find with Peter, John, and the rest of this early church is this: *the answer is found in the tribe.*

Strength in Numbers

Rather than send students into moments of great risk, isn't it better to keep them safe? Let's be honest; as youth leaders and parents, it terrifies us to put our students in positions where there is risk of any kind. Pursuing games, activities, teaching, and small-group communities inside the four walls of the church or home is by far the best place to create trust and dependence, right? Wrong. Safety-ism in our culture is a real thing and we are all prone to it. But creating great community is not about crafting great safe spaces inside youth group. It's not just about getting students inside the four walls of church. Tribes are created when students who dare to be bold invite the community of believers into their vision and it catches fire. I am not talking about gathering our students together so they can hang out in safety with their Christian friends. I am not talking about knowing some Christians across town and sitting at home praying for each other and doing nothing. The community I am talking about is one with no fear, one that is loud, and one that is bold.

Jewish authorities noticed Peter and John spoke with great boldness (Acts 4:13), and later the great multitude of believers prayed that they too would be bold (v. 29). That prayer was answered as the place where they were praying was shaken; they were filled with the Holy Spirit and continued to speak the word of God with boldness. The rest of the believers heard about what they did, praised God for it, and asked that they too could be filled and do what Peter and John did, and then it happened. But what is this boldness? What does it look like? Certainly, it is more than a willingness to shout out loud that they believed in Jesus.

The boldness of the community meant they were unashamed of Jesus; they did not try to use clever figures of speech or ambiguous examples so they could escape persecution. Instead they spoke plainly, confidently, and fearlessly. When we are confident in what we are saying, it is because we believe in what we are talking about. What I love about the believers in the early church is that they were interested in the truth of the gospel rather than how the gospel might make them look or what it might cost them. Imagine our students walking the halls of their schools with this kind of confidence. This kind of boldness cannot come by seeking community in a digital reality. We all need people in our physical space, caring for each other, praying for each other, and supporting each other. In every facet of life, there is strength in numbers. The ground can shake.

Making It Stick

If you are at all like me, you have sat back in your chair and thought about what it would be like to have a youth group that looked just like the local church, but too quickly dismiss it as impossible. While there are no guarantees, I have seen several groups of students who exemplify some common characteristics that seem to get them pretty darn close to the ideal. Here is what they do.

Establish a Tribe Early

A few months ago, I had a chance to meet a youth pastor who is changing the way community is created in church. We sat inside the church's café surrounded by kids playing on the church's indoor playground, in the middle of the week. In more than fifteen years of ministry, this was the busiest Thursday afternoon I had ever seen inside the church. He explained how important community was for them as a church. But every church says that, right? But for this church, community was more than just an idea, or goal, or even good intention. It was part of their DNA. They built this church in the community, for the community, and even by the community. It was largely one of the reasons for the playground in the first place. The surrounding community wanted one, so the church granted their wish. Now it's flooded with people all day long.

That same DNA flowed into their youth ministry. They recognized that many of their students had already established tribes by the time they entered high school—some as early as middle school. Whether it was sports, drama, music, even family; church and youth ministry were quickly moved down to the bottom of the list. They saw attendance suffer, commitments lacking, and retreats failing.

Their aim was to create community earlier. Instead of waiting until middle or high school to begin community groups, they started in fifth grade. Their research found that in fifth grade, students hadn't really found their tribe just yet, giving them an open door to establish youth ministry in the church as their tribe.

It's only been a few years, but their results show drastic improvement. Commitment levels among students are up, attendance is better, and they are having to turn students away from retreats because they are reaching capacity. It's simple: the earlier we introduce a student to his or her community within the church, the better chance we have of their making it their tribe.

Create Space for Real Community

You might not believe this, but if you ask your students to put their phones down or off and to be present in the moment, you will likely get an overwhelmingly positive response. Yes, our students are addicted. But as I noted earlier, it is a world they were born into, not one they chose. Students are beginning to see the benefits of putting the device down. They just don't know how. Mistakenly, we somehow think that our students ought to know better. They should know that devices aren't good for them, that they can't find true community through a screen, and that digital addiction can have life-altering effects. The truth is, they don't know. We have to teach them.

The kind of community God designed for us is no longer coming naturally to our students. We have to show them what it looks like to talk face-to-face, to look someone in the eye, and to carry on a conversation. There is almost a sense of relief for students when we specifically ask them to put their phones away. But we can't expect them to do it on their own. We have to show them, and over time they will experience the benefits of the community that develops—the kind of community that fosters incredible boldness for the gospel.

Seize the Opportunities God Grants You

Our students have a greater evangelistic opportunity than any of us adults. Daily, they enter a dark world full of sin. Our job as youth leaders, parents, pastors, and coaches is to effectively train them to take hold of every opportunity.

As I noted above, Peter and John could have healed the man and moved on; they could have sheepishly mentioned Jesus in hopes they wouldn't get in trouble, or obeyed the command to no longer speak the name of Jesus. Even in the presence of people of high rank, they did not take a backdoor approach to talk about Jesus. They offered no apologies for their belief and no sneaky solutions to get the gospel out. When told to refrain from speaking about Jesus, they did not retreat back to the church and hide, or sit back in their chair satisfied in their effort. They proclaimed the gospel, no smoke and mirrors, but plain and simple language that Jesus is the true Messiah of Israel, inaugurating His kingdom and a people greater than even the greatest of nations. Instead these young disciples grabbed hold of this opportunity to make sure as many people as possible would hear the gospel and experience God's grace through Jesus. Boldness and confidence to proclaim without apology or reservation the gospel of Jesus Christ in word and deed becomes the life blood of the community of believers, and to do so, we must rely on the Spirit's power rather than our own.

Imagine a youth ministry that prays as one body and mind, having the needs of each other and their community first on their minds at all times so that it becomes as vital as the air we breathe. That church needs to be here, and it needs to be now. And it can be, when we seize the opportunities God gives us. If we lack community, then we will lose our boldness. If we have no boldness, we have no real community.

Conclusion

As Israel crossed the Jordan River into the Promised Land, they were fully aware of what waited for them on the other side—foreign nations and enemies of Israel. They crossed, even knowing they were entering occupied land and conflict would soon follow. It wouldn't be long before Israel would square off with Jericho. God didn't just provide the means of crossing the river; He provided the means of becoming a people, a tribe, and a nation in a foreign land so they could be a light in the darkness and a city on a hill.

If we stay trapped in the solitude of our churches, circle of friends, and comfort groups, the gospel will reek of a self-serving savior and stories about what Christianity offers me and my interests. Isolation and silence create individualism. It becomes all about me, all about my world, and all about what my mind creates. But community creates sacrifice and a passion for the resurrection of all of God's creation. The gospel is no longer about me, but God and His mission. But just as Peter and John's confidence fed the rest of the community, so will the confidence of one feed your community, creating a unified group of believers boldly proclaiming the gospel together as one tribe.

FINDING A REASON

*People are generally better persuaded by the reasons
which they have themselves discovered than by those
which have come into the mind of others.*

Blaise Pascal

When I sat down at my computer to begin writing this chapter, I noticed my news feed was dominated by yet another public Christian figure declaring to have lost his faith. Marty Sampson, one of Hillsong's worship music writers, declared via Instagram he is genuinely losing his faith.[1] The Christian faith, according to Sampson, is no longer for him. His excuse: unanswered questions, the church ignoring important topics and key issues, and vague responses to lingering doubts. But let's be honest with ourselves: these kinds of stories are not new. Whether a public figure, a suburban mom, or the most popular kid in youth group, we have all heard the stories of people falling away from Jesus. Even the apostle Paul mentioned a few people who made the conscious choice to live life in a different direction (1 Tim. 1:19–20). Did they lose their faith? Did they really ever have it? Only Jesus really knows. But these very public professions of *unbelief* point out one key reality among many young Christians: many students really don't know why they believe what they profess to believe.

My Own Journey to Reason
Despite growing up in a loving home with great Christ-loving parents, I spent more than a decade actively pursuing a life apart from Jesus. My departure from the church in high school was much the same story we read in our social media news feeds as of late. As

with many students, sin easily captivated my attention. The culture of the 90s—plaid shirts, grunge rock, and our favorite *Friends* episodes—provided more than enough fuel to embrace the rebellious nature of teenage life. But despite the fresh challenges of a new 90s generation, it was the lingering questions left unanswered that allowed my doubts to become fully grown unbelief. I felt the church was ill-equipped to handle life beyond its walls; it was too legalistic, restrictive—unwilling to bend if it meant reaching more. I never found my tribe, never participated in youth group—more than that, I never found any reason to follow Jesus and live the life He desired for me.

It seemed clear to me that church had no place in my life after my elementary years. I was expected to obey because the Bible told me so. And I was expected to believe the Bible because the Bible told me so. Jesus, the resurrection, the wonders of grace, and eternal life in heaven were something not to be questioned. Honestly, I could have been Jonas in the opening chapters of Lois Lowry's *The Giver*. Life inside the church was programmed and predetermined. Don't walk outside the lines, don't question the methods; rules were to be taken seriously and followed meticulously. In the award-winning novel, Jonas seems content with a completely programmed life. Every aspect of life, from food, friends, job, family, even social interaction, is pre-scripted and programmed to achieve a certain desired outcome—the removal of free will and emotion. Only until he is assigned the role of Receiver did he discover the power of feeling.

So maybe my early faith experience wasn't quite that extreme, but raising questions about my faith, in my mind, was just as detrimental as Jonas's questioning the very existence of his world.

So I escaped. It would be ten years before God led me back to the same questions and ultimately back to Himself. I felt the pull to come back to the church, but this time I needed a reason to believe. What I discovered is what ultimately caused me not just to return to the church, but begin work in full-time ministry. I discovered there was sound evidence that God existed, the Bible could be trusted, and Jesus resurrected. I learned Jesus was the source for absolute truth, that hope could be found in Him, and despite the stain of sin in this world, God remains faithful. I fell in love with the discipline of Christian apologetics and dedicated my ministry to teaching these *reasons* to our youth.

I really didn't escape. But I do believe God provided me the space I needed to ask the necessary questions and truly discover a God who has made Himself known. But not a day goes by that I wish I didn't have had to endure the pain of sin, the consequences of some really dumb decisions, the relationships I damaged, and time I lost in my fog of stupidity. I see my journey in so many other students. They walk away, not because the pull of sin is too great or that culture has a more compelling story or better answers. They walk away because the culture is providing answers more readily.

Taking Inventory

After the news broke of our Hillsong friend Marty, many of my apologist friends were understandably frustrated. As apologists, we spend all our ministry efforts providing answers to some of the most vexing questions, giving believers and non-believers alike a steady stream of books, blogs, videos, and other resources to find their much-needed answers. Reasons are not impossible to find; we just have to know where to look.

No matter what you are doing in life, you have a reason. The job you take, the religious path you follow, the degree you pursue, the girl you ask out, even the movie you're planning to see this weekend—you have a reason for every one of them. Our relationship with Christ is no different. We have good reasons for believing Jesus is the risen Savior of the world. If your students have searched for the evidence, or they have experienced God in a profound and impactful way, their faith is likely standing on solid footing. But if their reason is, "That's what I grew up with," or "It just works for me," then they may be one doubt-filled crisis away from losing their faith.

You probably know that student. The one who is holding on to their faith for dear life. One wrong move and they are out. But they have questions. Lots of them. Perhaps you can answer some of them—maybe even most of them. But the wrong answer could have dire consequences. So we avoid the conversation, hoping the questions and doubts are more of a temporary inconvenience and not a crisis. We want our students to have an unwavering commitment and trust in who God is and the life He asks us to pursue, but we fear they have little reason to believe it.

My family and I have moved eleven times in about twelve years. I know, that's a lot. As difficult as it has been over the years, it has taught my family an important lesson. If you're packing it, you must have a reason to keep it. When you pack up a moving truck as many times as we have, you tend to take careful inventory of what you're packing. The less packing—and unpacking—the better. So each time we began to pack up the house, we carefully looked at each article of clothing, furniture, toy, appliance, and so forth, held it to the light, and asked ourselves, "Do I have a reason for owning this?" The stronger the reason, the more special the item became, the better we cared for it, and the longer we have it. Otherwise, we end up packing items in boxes, which get stored in the basement, garage, or attic never to be opened; and we soon forget we ever had it.

We fear our students won't hold on to their faith, that it won't stand the test of college life, family challenges, and their career; yet we neglect to help them form sound reasons, grounded in truth that not only help them maintain their faith in Christ, but propel their faith forward. It is almost as if we are afraid of taking faith and holding it up to the light to expose it, when all we are truly exposing is the hope within. If we allow our students to hang on to fear, we risk their boxing up their faith, letting it collect dust in storage next to countless other items once considered precious and valuable they now have no longer any use for.

Finding Hope

The good news is Christians are not asked to blindly follow Jesus, hoping that somehow it turns out to be true. In fact, it's quite the opposite. As Christians, we are called to always be ready with a reason for the hope we have in Christ (1 Peter 3:15). In other words, whatever our age, our season in life, or circumstances, we are required not only to know what we believe and why, but also to be able to give those reasons when called upon to do so. In the formidable minds of our teens, this command bears possibly even greater importance than the rest of us.

The apostle Peter, in his first letter, wrote to Christians who were scattered through Asia Minor and surrounding regions. Those new Christians found themselves in the midst of persecution for living faithfully in the kingdom of God, rather than the kingdom of Rome. Many had become social outcasts and needed direction in how to live as strangers in a hostile world—the same direction our students are asking the adults in their lives to give them.

The hope Peter referred to is the future resurrection that awaits Christians. The reason for hope is knowing beyond a shadow of doubt that because Jesus died and resurrected, the sin that causes death has been dealt with, the chasm between man and God had been bridged, and the promises God made all the way back in the Old Testament have been fulfilled in Jesus. Because Jesus resurrected, He will return to claim His kingdom and we, as His people, will rule with Him, and we have a reason to have hope.

It's not about the best arguments; it's not about winning people to our side; it's about hope. The hope of Jesus. The hope of restoration. The hope that someone can receive rest. The hope that someone gets to spend their eternal lives with their Creator. It's the hope that what once was broken and messed up and lost is now fixed and found. Everybody in some way, shape, or form wants hope. However, the origins of such a hope actually come just before the instruction to be ready—set apart Christ as Lord.

Wrestling with their faith, whether the questions come from a place of doubt within or from the skeptics they know in their lives, can be a fear-filled proposition. However, overcoming that fear begins with setting apart Christ as Lord. It's an intentional change in posture intended to create a reliance on Jesus as we help our students learn to look to Him for wisdom and guidance rather than to the world. When Christ is set apart as Lord, disciples are compelled to be ready with a reason, because the pursuit of discipleship guarantees questions are going to arise.

Creating a Culture of Questions

When I began my teaching career, I started each year asking my students to write about their reasons for believing—or in some cases, not believing—in Jesus. I never expected them to really articulate much of anything. Some managed to write some great reasons, but most were left repeating phrases they heard in their elementary years in church. But I was okay with that, because that wasn't the point. I didn't really intend for them to write much. The point was to simply create a specific kind of culture in my classrooms. I wanted to create a culture of questions.

Every one of your students has questions. There is no way around it, and there is no way of avoiding it, so please don't. Students need to feel a part of a community and culture where questions are encouraged and answered. Keep in mind there are students who have been raised to believe that to doubt and question is to have insufficient faith. However, questions and doubts can be incredibly productive when it leads to answers and certainty. Create a culture that encourages students to ask the tough questions and then explore answers together.[2]

The brain of a teenager is developing incredibly fast, taking in tremendous amounts of information at lightning-fast speeds. The faith many of our students were introduced to in elementary school changes almost overnight as they approach middle school.

Which, of course, creates a constant stream of questions that demand an answer. Although I don't have the space here to provide you with every answer to every question I can think of, I have created five categories of questions that I believe capture many of our students' top concerns when it comes to their faith.

Questions of Existence

It shouldn't come as much of a surprise that students may question the actual existence of God. Not necessarily on the grounds of a rational belief, but simply because the absence of a physical presence and the possible limited experience of Him would create the natural questioning of whether or not God is there. These kinds of questions from students are not much more than a sophisticated version of a young child's inquiry of God. Depending on the development of abstract thought, students at times will have difficulty wrapping their minds around the idea of God's existence.

As students get older, the question of existence becomes a question of origins and explanation. If somehow I can know God is there, then I can readily explain the existence of the universe, creation, my sin, mortality, and so on. If I can't know, then I am forced to rely solely on science for answers. Which, of course, is not only limited in its explanation of the universe, but will result in a series of answers far different from church. So you might see where questions of existence left unanswered can created a myriad of problems in the minds of our students. This creates a critical need to address these kinds of questions head on.

Questions of Plausibility and Reliability

There is no shortage of secular scholarship selling the notions that Jesus' resurrection was a hoax, the Bible cannot be trusted, and the Old Testament is nothing more than mythical tellings of an ancient people's understanding of the forces of nature. For example, Bart Ehrman, former Christian, New Testament scholar, and professor at the University of North Carolina, has argued extensively for many years that mainstream evangelical Christianity has Jesus all wrong. According to Ehrman, Jesus is not the Son of God, the Bible cannot be trusted as the inspired Word, and the resurrection belongs on the shelves next to other works of mythology.[3]

If our students don't know any better, scholars and authors like Ehrman sound convincing and can send even the most committed students into a faith crisis. But it doesn't take much digging to discover that Jesus is a real historical figure and there is plenty of data beyond the pages of Scripture and even other early Christian writings concerning Jesus. Similarly, what if we could know that the Bible is accurate and a reliable record of history and theology? It is. What if, despite the seemingly impossibility of the resurrection, the historical evidence actually showed Jesus rising from the dead three days after being put to death as the most likely scenario? It is.

If the Bible is going to be the ultimate source for truth in our lives and the lives of our students, then they need to be confident that what they read is actually true. Consider for a moment our culture's current moral condition. Our culture is overwhelmingly condoning and even celebrating sexual expression of every variety, while the Bible clearly condemns any sexual activity beyond what happens between a man and a woman inside the bond of marriage. Who are our students listening to? According to the Bible, sin has tainted every last thing, especially the hearts of humanity. Yet culture has unequivocally declared a belief in the inherent goodness of all people. Who our students believe will directly inform how they choose to live. When your students understand that what is in the Bible is a reliable source for truth, they are much more likely to live it out.

Questions Concerning Pain and Evil

Every time I ask students for questions about their faith, questions about pain, evil, suffering, and so on are always at the top of the list. Apologists commonly call this the problem of evil or the problem of pain. But the questions take all kinds of forms and originate from all types of people and circumstances.

"Why did God allow this to happen to me?"

"Why do bad things happen to good people?"

"If God exists, then how come there is so much evil in the world?"

"If God were good, then he wouldn't allow evil to exist, would he?"

The list seems endless. But these questions are generally either philosophical in nature or much more personal. It's the difference between asking, "Why does God allow evil?" and "Why did God allow my sister to be raped?" Allow students to ask the question and you'll quickly find a number of layers that often exist below the surface.

Questions of pain and evil can be—and often are—incredibly personal. And whether we realize it or not, ignoring the questions sends the clear message to our students that there is no answer. Perhaps God isn't in control after all, or worse, He doesn't care. Their solution is to find answers elsewhere because in their minds the church has failed them.

Maybe that slippery slope is a bit extreme. But to be sure, I want to stress the importance of pastoring our students through these kinds of questions. There are good answers for why there is evil, why some people experience incredible pain and suffering while others don't, and why God allows it all to happen.

Questions of Truth

Every time I have the opportunity to speak to a group of students on the topic of truth, I am always surprised at how engaged they are. It's almost as if they already know that culture is selling something they aren't willing to buy into just yet. They want to hear more. They want to make a more informed decision. I generally walk them through what truth is, the difference between subjective and objective truth, and why relativism doesn't work. The vast majority of students leave the room encouraged. Not only that truth exists, but that it can be known.

Questions of Depth

I had the privilege of teaching in schools that served many different denominations all at once. So at any given time, I could have a classroom of students from Baptist, Catholic, Lutheran, Pentecostal, non-denominational, Church of God, Church of Christ, and "I don't really know" churches. I learned that what can hold up the spiritual growth of our students are the deeper theological questions. It might be as complex as trying to understand the complexity of the Trinity, the debate about if one can lose their salvation, or the hypostatic union of Jesus. They are hard to learn and even harder to teach, but absolutely cannot be ignored.

Don't be afraid of going deeper with your students. We will get into this much more in the next chapter, but let me make a few comments here first. Never underestimate the ability of your students to think deeper and more critically. They are taught to do it in school, so when the church fails to connect a student's faith with their intellect, we are devaluing and de-prioritizing their faith. We absolutely must teach our students to connect the Christian worldview with education, politics, science, and history. One of the most straight-forward ways of doing so is introducing apologetics into your ministry and home life.

Moving Forward

On some level, I can understand and even appreciate the concerns and questions of Hillsong's Marty Sampson. But when you stop and think for a moment, reflect on the words of the apostle Peter, and explore the countless reasons we have for our hope in Christ, he has no excuse. As an adult he cannot rely solely on the church to supply him with every answer to every conceivable question.

However, as youth leaders, pastors, and parents, it is our God-ordained responsibility to help our students see not only that there are reasons, but to point them to the best possible resources. It's critical that we continue to educate ourselves, to search for the answers to our own questions and the questions of our students.

No, there is not an answer to every question. God is still a big mystery. But the Creator of all has given us more than we need to have the confidence necessary to walk in faith for what we hope for and be assured of what we cannot see just yet (Heb. 11:1). Israel's incredible moment crossing into the Promised Land was what seemed like an impossible task and the unknown on the other side terrifying. But the priests still picked up the Ark of the Covenant and stepped into the water, followed by one tribe after another crossing over on dry ground. Did they really just trust Joshua? Maybe, but wouldn't it be much easier to just call him crazy and wait for a more appropriate time to cross? Wouldn't it make so much more sense to find another way? In other words, what reason would Israel have for stepping out into such an incredible act of faith?

That moment wasn't the first time God had done something incredible among His chosen people. He used Joseph to keep Jacob's family alive through a dangerous famine by bringing them to Egypt. He rescued the nation of Israel after they had become slaves in Egypt. He provided an escape from Pharaoh through the Red Sea. He gave them everything they needed for their journey through the desert. Each moment, each provision, each lesson brought them closer and closer to the promise God had made them—a promise passed on from generation to generation. They would be a nation, they would have land, and they would be blessed so they could be a blessing to others. This was their promise. This was their hope. And God's work among them would be their reason to maintain the hope even in the darkest of situations, moments of exile, disobedience, and the unknown. The nation of Israel was ready to cross the Jordan because they had every reason to believe God would act and deliver on His promise, and so do we still today.

10
THINKING "CHRISTIANLY"

A Christian Education must primarily teach people to be able to think in Christian categories.

T.S. Elliot

A few years ago, I met a student named Drew. He was brilliant but incredibly lazy and quite possibly a professional skeptic. He had this signature way of sitting at his desk that told a greater story than even his words could. Slumped over, head resting comfortably in his hand, doodling on his paper; there was no one more disinterested in my discussions about Jesus. But Drew wasn't the only one. In fact, most of my students wanted little to do with learning about Jesus, God, theology, the Bible—you name it; if it had something to do with their faith, they couldn't have cared less. But put that same group of students in chapel or at a retreat and you would see them hands held high, worshipping with everything they have.

I pressed on. I continued to challenge Drew and his fellow students. Some of the parents caught wind of what I was trying to do. Initially, I was relieved, hoping that if I could gain the support of parents, perhaps I could reach the students a little faster and with greater success. Nope. Parents were losing their minds. For most of them, faith was not something that ought to be driven by intellect but by emotion. They were convinced that challenging students to think about their faith would create unnecessary doubt and frustration. Intellectual engagement was much too risky. "What if God is too difficult to understand and they walk away from their faith?" These parents were following Christ and raising their sons and daughters to be disciples from a place of fear. They thought if their students' faith would be allowed to enter and influence their secular sphere of life, it might not stand a chance.

Nearly every youth group faces the same challenge—fear that too great a challenge will drive them from Jesus rather than to Him. It comes as no surprise that there is an increasing number of students who lack even a simple understanding of the Bible. We can no longer assume students know who Moses, Abraham, Peter, and Paul are. The more post-Christian we become, the more we can't assume students can locate Bible books, chapters, and verses. Verse memorization is a thing of the past; the character of God, forgotten; critical thinking about matters of faith, ignored. It won't be long before youth ministry is working to reach students who have grown up in a home having never stepped into a church with very little or even no knowledge of Jesus. The solution has largely become the perpetual feeding of spiritual milk to our students. Teaching to the lowest common denominator comes with less risk—or so we have allowed ourselves to believe.

No Longer a Christian Mind

"There is no Christian Mind."[1] These are the first words written by Harry Blamires in his groundbreaking book, *The Christian Mind, How Christians Should Think.* In 1963, Blamires argued that although there is clear evidence for a Christian ethic, Christian practice, and Christian spirituality, we have left the work of the mind to the secular world leaving Christianity almost entirely dependent upon emotion. Today research is showing that the average Christian is not educated enough in terms of doctrine, practice, ethics, and virtue. Many Christians—our students included, to their detriment—believe that once they have professed faith, they are somehow automatically transformed. So there is no need to think deeper about God, theology, or the Bible. Christians are comfortable with chasing after the whims of emotional highs and lows. When things are good, it is time to sit back and relax.

But when times get tough, we seek the next emotional high from an event, conference, or worship experience. It may sound a bit harsh, but we have to ask ourselves, *Is this the faith experience we are passing on to our students?*

The age of enlightenment, a shift in philosophy, liberalism, postmodernism, and now post-truth ideology has successfully diluted education to the things that can only be considered scientific. In other words, only what can be tested and proved is worth knowing—what's left is a matter of opinion. High school graduates are leaving for college understanding evolution to be factual and morals to be relative, letting our students decide for themselves what they feel truth is. Where does that leave our students in how they *think* about the truth of their faith?

In their 2007 book, *UnChristian,* David Kinnaman and Gabe Lyons studied and chronicled the patterns of today's Christians as well as the thoughts about Christians from those outside the church community. When it came to the willingness and ability to think, "Outsiders believe Christianity insulates people from thinking. Often young people doubt that Christianity boosts intellect."[2] The consensus among people outside the walls of the church is that Christians are not only uninformed but encouraged to be brain dead, and most rejected the idea that Christianity is rational, relevant, or realistic. According to culture even more than a decade ago, Christians are not considered deep thinkers—a mentality that has seeped its way into how we disciple our students.

This trend has continued among GenZ. In Barna's recent study of the newest generation of students, they asked GenZ churchgoers about their perceptions of church and the Bible. Far too many young Christians see faith as something that is not the least bit intellectually stimulating or exciting. Part of that view comes from the increasing clash between faith and science. The majority of students see the Bible either in conflict with science (24 percent) or somehow refers to different aspects of reality (31 percent).[3] Almost no change from the views of the Millennials. When it comes to church, there continues to be a concerning amount of negative perceptions about it. The church is losing the battle for the mind.

Finding an Intelligent Faith

What Drew, his classmates, and their parents were actually afraid of was the idea of a faith that infiltrated and threatened their comfort with life and complacency of Jesus. This was made possible by a simple, almost childish faith. If they went too deep or knew too much, that would create greater responsibility. In some sense, ignorance is bliss. Part of their reasoning was that I was too focused on academics, creating a sterile faith not useful in their current lives. For them, it was less about their minds and more about their hearts. Allowing their biblical knowledge to go no deeper than simple devotionals and elementary stories with the occasional spiritual and emotional high would never prepare them to successfully engage their world with the gospel. How can we expect students to enter a post-Christian culture without a full and mature knowledge of Jesus? How will they make mature decisions without a Christ-like mind?

I'm all for emotionally charged worship and that overwhelming feeling of the Spirit of God moving through a room; the kind that gives you goose bumps, tears in your eyes, and the undeniable need to create spiritual movement. I love being at youth conferences and witnessing firsthand Spirit-filled worship, students coming to the front to give their lives to Jesus, and tears of joy flooding a room. Worship has a way of capturing our imagination and transporting us to the throne room of God. It's a sight that I never get tired of. But what informs that emotion? What informs the love that our students so boldly proclaim? It's their mind and the depth of their knowledge of God. It's easy to forget in our emotionally driven culture that there is an intellectual core to our Christian faith. It's impossible to love God without a desire to understand more about Him.[4] Remember that the greatest command is to love God with all our heart, soul, *mind*, and strength (Matt. 22:37, author's emphasis).

Think about the movies your students watch, the music they listen to, their searches on the Internet, conduct at school, or even their perception of events around the world. Do they filter those things through a Christian worldview? Or do they allow them to shape their worldview? Now, think about how you approach these with your students. Let me show you what I mean. Below are a few examples from popular culture. As you read, think about how your students have responded or are responding now with a biblical worldview framework.

Parkland

On February 14, 2018, a gunman opened fire killing seventeen people at Marjory Stoneman Douglas High School in Parkland, Florida. In the hours and days following, the nation paused—to watch, listen, and pray. But if you're a parent, pastor, or youth leader, you likely remember Sandy Hook, Virginia Tech, and Columbine. All of these stirred up something inside us—the desire to do something and to change something. But I think the recent Parkland shooting created the possibility for a much greater response. Parkland didn't just initiate a response from adults, like parents, politicians, and teachers; it initiated a response from students—who took to their most powerful tool—social media.

Only weeks later, thousands of students across the nation sought social change by organizing a national school walkout. Spurred on by the tragedy in Parkland, students' safety in schools became a primary, nationwide focus. Naturally, such an act raised all kinds of questions. Should we be allowing students to walk out of school? Should students be featured on national television and given a platform for their cause? Should students be taking to social media with a "whatever it takes" mentality to create the change they seek?

I spent some time tracking the opinions from pastors and parents across the country and found the widest possible range of perspectives. Some were thrilled to see students actively involved and standing up for what they believe in. With so much student apathy, it is almost refreshing to see the exact opposite. Others found it easy to question their motives and intentions. Are they seeking social change for the good of humanity, or are they just trying to be noticed, get on TV, or merely get out of classes for a few days?

Now consider how your students have responded to the things like the gun debate, protests, and school safety. Who is shaping their opinion? If the church does not intentionally speak into these issues—and others like it—students will be easily distracted and swayed by news and social media.

You Need to Calm Down

If you haven't heard the name Taylor Swift, you likely are living under a rock. The singer songwriter is quickly becoming one of the most influential voices in the music industry. She doesn't rely on quippy tweets or racy Instagram posts. Instead, she masterfully leverages quite possibly the most effective tool in shaping the minds of youth—music. Although I don't consider myself one of her millions of fans, I do respect her songwriting skills, catchy and energetic music, and her commanding stage presence. She is no doubt GenZ's Madonna.

Although catchy and certainly enjoyable, Taylor Swift's music is intent on sending a message. One of her most popular singles, "You Need to Calm Down," looks to send a wonderful message of love and acceptance and that we all just need to take a step back and not give in to all the political, religious, and ideological fighting that is taking place in our country. At first listen, I was in hearty agreement. That was until I saw the video and dug a bit deeper into what Swift was actually selling. In pure secular cultural style, Swift confuses love and acceptance with complete affirmation and moral dissolve. The song is actually a dig at conservative values, calling out specifically the evangelical Christian view that the behaviors within the LGBTQ community are sinful—we need to "calm down." In fact, the song is so much geared toward activism that proceeds from the song's sales support the LGBTQ community.

It's easy to ignore it, but stop and consider what our students are listening to, watching, and the video games they are playing. Sure, the ratings system is helpful, but it's not exactly designed to sniff out worldview and political agendas. We have to teach our students to hear it and properly filter it.

Silence of the Lambs

About a year ago, I was having lunch with a youth pastor friend of mine who works in the suburbs of Chicago. I wanted to hear about some of the specific and biggest challenges he was facing. He told me that in his twenty years of youth ministry, he has never seen his students be so silenced as they are right now. He told me a story of a girl who desperately wanted to be a part of the drama department. But to be a part of the school's plays and other various performances you had to be openly bisexual. Sexual experimentation was an unwritten prerequisite. When the other students in the department found out this girl was a Christian and actively involved in youth group, they immediately ostracized her, while teachers and administrators remained quiet and uninvolved in the matter.

Convinced this was an isolated incident, I pressed for more evidence. I shouldn't have asked. He told several more stories of a similar nature. Each one was more disturbing than the next: teachers suppressing biblical views on history and science; students left out of friend groups for sharing the gospel; even Jackie, another student, was shamed into depression because she realized she really wasn't attracted to other girls. Even with his twenty-plus years of experience, he struggled with how to help students respond.

117

The one thing each of these stories has in common is, in some form or other, students are being forced to respond. Ignoring or hiding becomes less and less of an option, requiring our students to be mature in their thinking and to be able to, as T. S. Elliot noted, "think in Christian categories." As leaders of youth, we have an important decision to make. Either we ignore the cultural influences surrounding our youth and hope the emotional highs and Sunday school lessons are enough, or we stand with our students and guide them through events, music, movies, politics, and social pressures so they can meet these challenges head-on with a Christian worldview, thereby actually strengthening their faith for the continued journey ahead. The reality is our students need more than just an intelligent faith; they need a mature faith.

Our students are up against secularism, skepticism, and alternative forms of spirituality, and they lack the context for how to infiltrate and transform their world with the gospel. Houston Baptist professor and author Nancy Pearcey says it this way, "The reality is that most students lack the sense of how Christianity functions as a unified, overarching system of truth that applies to every area of life. Instead, they hold to Christianity as a collection of truths, but not as Truth."[5]

Achieving *Telos*

I didn't give up on Drew, the class, or their parents. I'm pretty stubborn, so I dug my heels in deeper. I was convinced if I could just reach my goal, drag them through the rest of the year, they would see what I was at least trying to do. A year went by; they were still quite skeptical. Two years passed; they loosened their grip a little bit. By year three, my efforts to infuse a more intellectual faith into their already vibrant, emotionally-driven experience of Jesus began to pay off. They were getting it because they were witnessing the benefits and exponential growth in their students. The fear of what might happen to their students' faith was overshadowed by the anticipation of what could happen *through* their students' faith.

A strong intellectual faith, coupled with parents' and students' desire for emotional moments, became the beginning of a formula that I soon required anywhere I taught. I had four specific goals I was after to make my students more mature Christians who think "Christianly":

- Create a greater excitement for God and a deeper appreciation for their salvation.
- Help students successfully deal with doubt and questions.
- Make worship more intense and emotional.
- Prepare students to be able to not only engage culture but transform it.

Much of traditional learning in the past has followed the common pattern of head, heart, hands. The idea is if we can teach the mind, it will lead to a change of heart, and thereby create an outworking of one's hands. Past generations swore by this method. In fact, a lot of my learning about teaching had this model in mind. However, it has a tendency to focus too much on ,teaching to the left side of the brain and largely ignore the right side—hoping it will catch up. For Millennials and GenZers, this model seems quite a bit backward and counterintuitive. My goal was never to produce faith in students exclusively academic in nature. To the contrary, my goal was to connect experience and emotion with intellect; to connect creativity with logic; connecting the right side of the brain with the left. My goal was to create students with a mature faith, "attaining to the whole measure of the fullness of Christ" (Eph. 4:13), who take captive every thought and make it obedient to Christ (2 Cor. 10:5), and who are transformed by the renewing of their minds (Rom. 12:2).

The path to students who have a mature faith—one that transforms their world—must pass through the process of becoming a thinking Christian—a lesson drilled into the early church's DNA by the apostle Paul. Even a church as challenged as the first century church in Corinth was, Paul knew for them to reach the unity and love required of the church they had to be able to properly filter the world's sin and standard through a biblical matrix. This was a church dealing with significant sexual sin, jealousy, and division. A complete all-around misunderstanding of what a holy, Christ-centered life looked like in practice.

Whether it was the church at Corinth, Ephesus, Philippi, or Rome, Paul generally had the same goal in mind—to be a complete disciple, fully mature, and fully contributing to the body of Christ. Paul's letter to Ephesus reminded the church that the gifts God gave each believer were designed to be used to prepare them for works of service, so that the body might be built up until everyone reached unity in the faith and in the knowledge of the Son of God and became mature, attaining to the church's greatest capacity for growth (Eph. 4:12–14). Just like Jesus, Paul is calling believers to fully realize their intended purpose in the kingdom. You guessed it—it's that word *telos* again. Most translations use *mature*, but the actual word Paul uses is *telos*. The goal is to reach unity in the faith and in the knowledge of Jesus reaching our intended goal as individuals and as the church.

If students understood more about God, they would naturally gain a greater appreciation for Him, and, therefore, a deeper love for Him. I remember trying to show students how much better devotional time could be if they knew more context, more characteristics of God, and had a better grasp on the nature of salvation.

Plumbers or Philosophers?

After those first three years, parents and students were asking for more, to go deeper. Worship was better, service more heartfelt and genuine, and love for God and neighbors grew by leaps and bounds. All according to plan. But the last goal ended up being more of a happy accident. I began to understand that truly great discipleship does not—in fact, cannot—stay locked inside the person. It might be a personal transformation, but it's designed to create incredible transformation for the world around them. The church is in great need of this exact kind of disciples—the ones who can transform their culture. Some of us are content with accepting the way the world is and finding a way to get along, so long as we are becoming a better person. But personal growth gives us a clearer insight into the biblical picture of the way the world should be and live to create that world right here, right now.

Who would we rather our students be? Our culture won't be changed by our hearts' good intentions, nor will it be changed by simply thinking. In his book, *Culture Making: Recovering Our Creative Calling*, Andy Crouch suggests the church needs more plumbers rather than philosophers, more artists and artisans, and fewer abstract thinkers. In our efforts to engage culture, we spend too much time thinking about worldviews and overanalyzing culture rather than changing it.[6] Crouch is right. We need students who are discipled into being plumbers, cultural practitioners working to create a culture that mirrors the kingdom of God. We need students who live in their world for the sake of their world.

Imagine the impact of our students as plumbers. Philosophers can successfully breakdown Taylor Swift songs, decipher their meaning, and make a sound personal choice if listening to her music is a Jesus choice or not. But plumbers know how to transform their culture by engaging their peers with the song, finding ways through its popularity to discuss and communicate truth. Philosophers take to social media to proclaim their disgust with school shootings and to—perhaps somewhat passively—pursue reform. Plumbers dig deeper into their own school and find ways to love their fellow students, to eliminate bullying, and to create a stronger school community. Philosophers gather like-minded people around them, so they wax eloquently about the majesty of Christ, avoid suppression and silence by avoiding those with different opinions. Plumbers look to build relationships with different people. They build bridges, find common ground, and build trust, giving them the right to share the truth of Jesus to those who normally refuse to hear it.

Philosophers pontificate about truth; plumbers transform their culture with it.

Making It Stick

Most of us older people have learned along the way the concept of head, heart, hands. Ideally, if we understand something, it has the power to change our heart, and therefore how we act. This was precisely the sort of pedagogy I learned while in seminary. There's just one problem. It's backward. At least it is for Millennials and GenZers. Younger Christians actually learn by experience first, meaning their experience in church, how faith is expressed in families, how their non-Christian friends perceive their faith, and their experience in sharing it with others. Their hearts will align with the experience and inform their minds in how they ought to think.

This doesn't mean we ignore our minds. I hope by now you have seen its importance. Nor does it mean we prevent students from ever experiencing the world as it is for fear their faith might be challenged. Instead we aim to create a holistic approach seamlessly integrating experience with emotion and with the mind. Each informing the other. It means allowing creativity, relationships, and knowledge to capture the imagination of our students that moves them into mature discipleship.

There are many ways to make this happen. But I have three that can work at dinner, in youth group, or with a small group meeting.

Learn from Experiences

The first practice after a Friday night football game was Saturday morning practice. The goal wasn't to run, or hit, or go over plays. The day after practice was designed for two specific things: to lick our wounds and watch game film. We needed to rest, but more than that, we needed to see as soon as possible what we did right and what we did wrong. We learn by doing, making mistakes, and correcting those mistakes—our brains are wired that way. So when you think of experiences to grow your students into mature thinking Christians, they need the space to try, to succeed, to fail, to review how it unfolded, and learn from the experience.

But that's not all. Students still have to go to school, participate in sports, music, or other activities. Likely those things occur in the real world. It's great that students can retreat back into church or among Christian friends for some feel-good worship and motivational teaching. But what if that time could also be used for debriefing, sharing victories, and defeats? What if students could re-enter their world with useful tactics?

But this isn't only about their experiences outside the church. As leaders and parents, we need to consider the experience inside the church as well. If you haven't yet had a student come to you in confidence and reveal they are living a transgender lifestyle, you will, and soon. How we respond to sin is critical in crafting the kind of experience that matures their faith without compromising truth.

Theological Training

There is genuine excitement that comes from wrestling with God. There is a certain satisfaction that comes from a faith driven by an intense desire to understand Him. Such depth comes only from the discipline of theological study. But I can almost hear what you're thinking. You don't need to be a professional theologian to be a disciple. You don't need a seminary degree or to read old, dusty books on exegetical fallacies or multi-volume commentaries—although the theology nerd in me would suggest that you do. Certainly, we cannot expect our students to dive that deep—although some will. Can they really handle such complex ideas? Yes, and they want to, because we are all theologians—because we all think about God and live accordingly. No matter what level our students enter the journey, it begins when they desire to seek a deeper understanding of who God is and what it means to put their trust in Jesus. What we think about Jesus informs how we feel about Him and how we live out that belief.

How and what our students think about God plays a critical role in their journey as a disciple. Learning to think "Christianly" enables informed Christian action. Theology sets the foundation for our desire to want to see things in a Christian way. Students' study of theology helps them make judgments about how best to act; it encourages them to engage with the real world.[7] In other words, theology is our discipleship in action. So don't be fearful of introducing more complex ideas about God, salvation, theological history, and even some of the differences in theology among Christians, because we can't imagine the deepest possible love for God without the greatest possible understanding of Him. You likely know the theological level of understanding in your students. Raise the bar. They will meet it, and in the end, thank you for it.

Cultivate Creativity

About ten years ago, we sounded the alarm because the Millennial generation was leaving the church in droves with no sign of return. The church tried being more relevant, created big events and the superstar youth pastor. Maybe better music would work, we thought. Or perhaps better games, and exchanging exegetical sermons for motivational speeches would do the trick. Over the last decade, none of these things has made a positive impact on discipling our students. Instead, what we discovered was that in our efforts to create specific spaces for teens—to accomplish these new-fangled goals—we siloed our youth off from the rest of the church. But what does youth leaving the church have to do with creativity?

God has gifted each of us—students included—with the ability to create. The church ought to be a place where that creativity is birthed and nurtured. But that can't happen for students who have no place in the wide sphere of the church community because they have been separated since birth.

Conclusion

While it certainly is not a guaranteed fix or some kind of secret formula to highly effective disciples, helping students think in Christian categories helps them to create a framework of how both sides of their brain can work in concert to best represent God and His kingdom. It helps join together creativity and logic and puts it into action. In our final chapter, we will dissect specifically how our students' creativity can make an immediate impact in the church as well as how they interact with the world in the years to come. So let's take a look at how we begin to train students to be plumbers.

11
CREATED TO CREATE

You can be creative in anything—in math, science,
engineering, philosophy—as much
as you can in music or in painting or in dance.

Sir Ken Robinson

During my first years of ministry, I had a bit of an attitude problem. I felt since I was pursuing a seminary degree my church should somehow automatically let me teach and preach sermons. Yeah, I was a little arrogant. I remember sitting in my pastor's office, essentially complaining that I wasn't getting the respect I thought I deserved. As he patiently listened, he smiled, walked over to his desk, grabbed his Bible and started thumbing through it. I didn't pay much attention to what he was doing until he cut me off mid-sentence, handed me his Bible and said, "Read this."

I was a seminary student, I thought, so who was he to hand me a passage of Scripture like I hadn't heard of it? In fact, I was certain that I probably dissected the passage in Greek. But I read it anyway. I read it begrudgingly, but I read it. After I finished, we talked about it for a bit. I nodded as if I understood and appreciated the time and insight. Truth is, I left that room not fully grasping what God was trying to teach me.

As I finished my degree and matured in ministry, I came back to the passage over and over. It haunted me. It was like God would not let me forget it until I learned the lesson I needed to learn. I caught it when I finished my first year of teaching.

With Great Power Comes Great Responsibility

The passage is about a master who takes a journey (Matt. 25:14–30). But before he leaves, he entrusts his servants with varying amounts of his wealth to manage. Most of the servants manage what the master entrusts to them by making wise investments and getting a worthwhile return for their efforts. But one of the servants decided to do something different. Instead of investing, out of fear he buried what was entrusted to him. Naturally, when the master returns, he is thrilled with all the servants but the one. Why? Because he failed to take proper care with what he was given. It wasn't his, but his to manage. The master not only strips the lazy servant of what little he does have but gives the others more.

I struggled in my early days of ministry, not because I was arrogant or felt I wasn't being respected (okay, I was, and I did), but because I didn't have a grasp on what God had given me, how I should invest it, and how it would contribute to the kingdom. I had a hard time finding my place within the church and finding community. The struggle ended up creating unnecessary tension and resentment toward others who were serving, my pastors, and even the church as a whole. I saw no reason to invest because I had little clue as to what I could offer.

Here's the thing—many of our students feel the same way. But you probably do a spiritual gifts inventory or have skillfully identified the musical students, the outgoing ones, the techy ones, and the creative ones. So that's good, right? Not quite. While those certainly help and you could add in a Meyers-Briggs personality test, a DISC assessment, or everyone's new favorite Enneagram—none of these are getting to the root of what my pastor was trying to teach me. Of course, there is nothing wrong with having students sign-up to be greeters, leading worship in the band, or working the soundboard. In fact, there is a ton right with those things. The more you get students engaged and invested in your community, the higher degree of commitment you're going to receive.

But what do you do with the introverted kid, the math kid, the writer, or the computer nerd? It slips past us when we aren't looking, but if a student can't contribute somehow to the production of youth group time, and they don't want to shake hands and smile at the newcomers, then we rest contently while they passively sit in a chair for the evening. For many of us, that is where our gifts assessment ends. Why concern ourselves if the student's gift doesn't fit into the context of youth group?

Because if we don't help students walk this path, they will be missing a key piece of discipleship—investment. Jesus tells the story because He knows how easy it is to accept Jesus as Lord and Savior, then sit back and do nothing. It's easy to make excuses for why we can't evangelize, why our churches aren't growing, and why we aren't making a difference in our communities, schools, and families. It's easy to be the wicked, lazy servant. I actually think that for some of us, it's not all that difficult to sympathize with him just a little bit. But as we work to grow our students spiritually into mature disciples, there are three truths I want to give you which will help steer us clear from the attitude and fear of the wicked lazy servant.

Students Are Creative

It's incredible to think God created each one of us uniquely in His image. When you look at the variety of personalities, gifts, and physical traits of a person, it's hard to wrap our minds around the creativity of God. It's not just that God is the Almighty Creator, but He is also creative. Everything you can touch, taste, smell, see, and hear, came out of the creative mind of God—from nothing. Everything we know—and the stuff we haven't even discovered yet—originated from the divine creative mind. But there is something far too many Christians seem to forget—or perhaps never learned.

We are co-creators with God. We have been created to create. Think about it. In the creative mind of God, He knew before the foundation of the world that humanity would need to create cities, governments, and economies. He knew there would be a need for teachers, doctors, lawyers, writers, artists, construction workers, and mathematicians. He knew humanity would invent cars, planes, computers, and the internet. And because we are created in His image, every good thing we create has a divine imprint.

This is part of the job God gave Adam all the way back in the Garden of Eden in Genesis. Adam was called to do more than just consume the benefits of God's created order. He was commanded to care for it and participate in it. God put Adam in a position as co-creator with God. Even the command to be fruitful and multiply is a command to create and be creative. We may not be in the Garden, but the mandate has not changed. Every one of our students—whether they consider themselves creative or not—is in fact, creative. In whatever way God has gifted them, what they are passionate about and just really good at, they have the divine mandate to use who they are in Christ to be creative. However, our students may not be keenly aware of what that could look like for them, so it's our job as youth leaders and parents to help them discover and walk that path.

Students Have a Craft

Let's return to the master and his servants. I think it's easy to wonder just a little why the master was so upset with the last servant. He didn't lose any money, and he gladly returned what was originally given. *It's about potential.* What the master gave each servant had incredible potential. In fact, the master never intended for the servants to just maintain his wealth, the intention was to multiply it. Each of the servants held more than just the master's wealth; they held and were given responsibility over potential wealth. So when the lazy servant buried his portion out of fear, the master actually suffered a net loss, because he lost what could have been.

Whether you prefer to quote Voltaire or Uncle Ben Parker from *Spider-Man*, "*with great power comes great responsibili-*

ty." Our students have each been given incredible gifts with infinite potential—gifts designed to reflect the image and glory of God and further His kingdom. But if all we are recognizing are the skills of the kid who plays guitar or the one who can run the soundboard, then we are burying any potential the rest of our students would have had.

Therefore, we have to help our students discover their creative calling and fully realize their potential to take who they are, what they love, and what they can create—and how they can uniquely point others to Christ. Their creative ability is innate to the image of God in them. How that is revealed is designed to be directly reflective of who God is. Not only should we help students realize their gifts, but also help them fully invest and tap into their unlimited potential.

They All Have a Canvas

The impact our students can make with their gifts can be felt on two levels. The first is internal. We have talked about holiness, *telos*, renewal, and resurrection—all very important factors when talking about discipleship. However, it's the life we have been given, the talents we have received, and the responsibilities we bear that serve as the canvas on which discipleship is played out. In other words, God has asked all of us to be disciples by being holy and fully realizing our intended purpose as people created in His image, but we show what that looks like through what we love, what we are good at, and the people in our lives. The same is true for our students.

If you struck up a conversation with me, it wouldn't take long to discover that I am not a math guy. I don't like it. I'm not good at it. For whatever reason, my brain just isn't wired to speak that language. So as a teacher, I would often joke about math being evil. That was until a student of mine named Tony wrote a brilliant paper. In fact, it was so good that it was published in a book I wrote, featuring several students.[1] He argued that there are only two things we know of considered to be necessarily existent. Which basically means, something is existent in and of itself, nothing created it. It just is. Those two things are math and God. The basic idea goes like this: two plus two is four. It always has been, always will be. Nothing created that; it's necessarily existent. The idea was that if math and God are existent in the same way, and much of the universe we can explain using math, then perhaps math is the language of God. Well, that was enough to stop me from calling math evil, to say the least.

It's one thing to see the youth band's worship leader, using her life as a canvas to showcase the creative work of God Almighty. Maybe she listens to worship music, writes a few of her own songs, and even sees the deeper theology behind the music. But it's another thing to see how Tony found a way to showcase God's creative work through math. Tony found how math could be creative and be his canvas.

We need more students like Tony, and we need more leaders to recognize that kind of creative ability. Instead of math, maybe it's a knack for business, acting, history, woodworking, engineering, or even baking cookies. These are the makings of the masterpieces God is at work creating in and through your students.

Culture Making

If we are asking our students to realize and invest their talents for the movement of the gospel and for leaders to come alongside and help, then what exactly is the expected outcome? If all students (in fact, everyone) are incredibly creative because God is creative, then what are we asking them to create? In other words, how do their gifts translate into something creative? What should that look like?

What I am suggesting is something I learned from Andy Crouch's book, *Culture Making*. In it, he argues the only way to truly change culture is to create it. In the book, Crouch identifies the most common ways Christians typically address and interact with culture—critiquing, consuming, or copying culture—which he calls postures.[2] If you take a look at any youth ministry around the United States, you will no doubt find a group advocating for one of these postures. But significant problems arise when our critique of culture too often leads to an unhealthy avoidance or complete condemnation of culture. Simply consuming culture can lead us down a path that compromises the biblical standard, or when we try to copy culture, it creates a comfortable Christian subculture sheltering our students from engaging the wider culture with the gospel.

Instead of allowing ourselves and our students to be forced into an unhealthy posture and attitude toward the wider culture, Crouch suggests a biblical approach taken straight from the earliest pages of Genesis. Crouch says we should take the posture of creators and cultivators, or perhaps, artists and gardeners.[3] Basically, these two are insistent on engaging the world as it is and working with it wisely, "making the most of what is beautiful and weeding out what is distracting and useless."[4] They are intently using their gifts and creativity to tend to God's created order as people created in His image. This is precisely the posture that will create the space and freedom for our students to not only engage their culture but to create it.

There is no group more tapped into and engaged with culture than our students, so they must be ready to do more than just survive in it; they must contribute to and create culture. But imagine the impact our students could make now, and in the future, if they understood what it meant to be an artist or a gardener, to make the best of what culture provides, weed out what is useless, and create something that glorifies the King and broadens the reach of His kingdom. Imagine the effects of students creating culture saturated with the gospel.

It's not a perfect science, and there aren't really any simple steps to take to make this happen. However, as leaders, it begins with opening our eyes to the reality that every student is creative, every student is gifted, and every student bears the responsibility of investing that gift. Doing so will change how we walk with our students and guide them as they discover just how God has wired them and what it looks like to live it out. Some students will already know it, some will identify something quickly, and others will struggle for several months or even years before they fully grasp God's creative calling. But stick it out with them.

Conclusion

We have come a long way. We began by taking a step back and making sure our students understood the journey. We put our toes in the water, kept our eyes on Jesus, and despite what looked like an impossible task, trusted God and crossed the river. We led our students to the opposite bank into a foreign land and began to see what discipleship in another world would look like. The journey with our students does not end with the final pages of this book. It continues on. Culture will change, the landscape of youth ministry will change, but our goal of making disciples who make disciples carries on.

The story of Israel as the people of God did not end on the opposite shore of the Jordan River in Jericho. The journey was only beginning. Keep reading the Old Testament, you find countless mistakes, unbelief, and the damaging effects of continued sin. God showed up time and again in incredibly miraculous ways, and yet Israel continued to flounder. But God never failed to deliver on His promise. The same is still true today. Despite the incredible challenges before them, there is nothing that can separate our students from the love of God in Christ Jesus (Rom. 8:38–39). We are asking our students to live against the grain, stand in opposition, and boldly proclaim the gospel. We are asking them to risk popularity, social status, and relationships. But we are also inviting them to cross a river—do what seems unthinkable—to witness God do the unbelievable.

We began with Israel's journey into the land God promised. Allow me to finish with the city He has promised to come. John described his vision of the new city of Jerusalem coming down from heaven, "It shone with the glory of God and its brilliance was like that of a very precious jewel, like a jasper, clear as crystal" (Rev. 21:11). The city will be surrounded in gold, illuminated by the glory of God, and the river of life flowing straight through it (Rev. 22:1–2). This is the land we wait for, the city we will live in. It's the end of the journey. So parents, pastors, leaders, and coaches, take every minute and every opportunity to get beyond the edge of the water and into the Promised Land—the New Jerusalem.

CONCLUSION

No matter how old you are, how many students you lead, or how long you've been involved in student ministry, the process of making disciples seems more difficult with each passing year. So for the seasoned parent and the rookie youth pastor, I hope you feel more prepared, more confident, and have a few more strategies to use as you think through how to best reach the rising generation.

Throughout this book I have talked quite a bit about the challenges we face with our students, Western culture and the post-Christian world we live in. And I am confident that we have met those challenges head-on while standing firm on biblical convictions. But it is far too easy to get down on the next generation. Let's be honest; it's almost a reflex to think of a new generation as somehow being less than the generations before. If you're old, like me, it's easy to look at students and label them as lazy, unconcerned with the future, unmotivated, not as smart, too soft, and so forth. But to the contrary, I sincerely believe there is an incredible hope with the rising generation.

And that's how I want to close this book. With hope. The hope we have for the next generation as we help them pursue Jesus. Yes, there are challenges. Big ones, in fact. But there is also an incredible opportunity, optimism, and most of all, hope. Let me show you what I mean. Here are nine hope-filled characteristics of the next generation.

They are after authenticity.

If you work with students, then you know. You know they see right through us adults when we are trying too hard. The older I get, the more I can see that students really just want real. They want authentic, original, credible, and trustworthy adults they can count on. They are constantly surrounded by fake news, misinformation, conflicting reports, and opinions expressed as fact. The more information, the more confusion—and they are starting to see right through it. Give them real, and you will gain their trust.

They desire close communities.

There is a lot of discussion and research trying to determine whether or not the world of social media is creating greater connections or a greater chasm in interpersonal relationships. Only a generation ago we had to learn how to communicate in a digital world; today, students need to learn how to communicate in the physical world. But regardless of how our methods of communications have changed, our need to be connected is still very much a thing. And just from what I have seen over the last few years, the shift in how our students communicate and relate to one another has highlighted this need maybe more than in previous generations. In other words, I think students are starting to see the need for what most of us grew up with—close community interaction. A tribe.

They are multi-cultural.

Growing up, I understood diversity as an abnormality I saw only in textbooks. I lived with, played with, and went to school with people just like me. Diversity was intentional and out of the ordinary. But our students today are growing up in a more diverse culture than any previous generation before them. So much so that there is a new normal. Multi-cultural communities, families, schools, and so forth, are not only expected, but normal.

They may not consider themselves ready for adulthood, but they are looking for us to be examples.

This almost seems counterintuitive, but the more I look at it, the more I see this as true. Students are taking less risk, are more dependent on parental involvement prolonged often through college, and, based on when they are getting married and starting families, are far less in a hurry to enter into what Americans traditionally think of as adulthood. However, they are looking to adults to give them a clear and positive picture of what adulthood looks like—from family responsibility, jobs, integrity, marriages, parenting, even what we wear.

They want to be successful.

Millennials became well known for their desire to do work that mattered. They didn't just want a job; they wanted a career that had a purpose greater than themselves. And that birthed an explosion of start-up companies focused more on giving back than having a significant bottom line—and their contributions have continued to have a lasting socio-economic impact. While GenZ may not have the same philanthropic focus as Millennials, they still have their sights set on success. Yes, it is true. It might seem like a miraculous act of God to unglue their eyes from their gaming and social media, but our students are seeking financial success—and that success can be useful for business growth, churches, non-profits, and the overall economy.

They are willing to work.

Work may look a little different, but that does not mean they are not ready to get their hands dirty. My dad has always been a machinist. Which means, growing up, I learned the trade—however brief it was. Those days taught me incredible lessons of hard work, determination, meeting deadlines, working a whole eight-hour day, and problem-solving. While I doubt many students are flooding the oily floors of the local machine shop, many of these same lessons are being learned in their digital world. It looks different, but the lessons often translate.

They are open to conversations about spirituality, Jesus, and truth.

I have a few talks on truth that I have had the opportunity to give from time-to-time to groups of students. It never fails. Every time

I do, students are completely engaged and captivated. We talk about truth, relativism, and our post-truth culture. It always ends in a flood of questions and further discussion—sometimes for an hour or more after the event. I am pretty sure it is not me but their desire to know more than what culture or even the church has taught them about truth and reality.

They are genuinely seeking ways to love others.

Given the world they are connected with, the diversity they experience daily, and the moral uncertainty of our culture, this is a group of youth determined to love others. They may not be entirely sure of what that looks like, or how to express the love of Christ to those we disagree with, but they are determined to figure it out.

They want a voice and to know how to use social media to leverage it.

Each morning I open my social media feeds to catch up with the world, see what is trending, and how I might engage. Pick your platform of choice, and there is no shortage of students making their opinions known. In their minds, the world is not *going* to be theirs soon. It *already* is. They have the means to have a voice, and they know how to use it.

These are opportunities, not guarantees. As leaders and mentors of the next generation, it is our job to leverage these opportunities to grow their faith and move the gospel forward by allowing students the space to experience Christ in a way that not only changes their lives but the lives of those around them.

So that's it. My hope is that these pages have been a source of inspiration, instruction, and what will become innovation inside your ministry or family. But this incredible process of discipling our students cannot end with this book. None of us can afford to go to sleep tonight with nothing more than good intentions. We need movement forward. So pick just one thing. Go back and review if necessary, and pick at least one thing from the Making

It Stick sections to work on. What can you implement this week, month, or year? What is at least one thing you know you need to change in your ministry or family to create deeper, more impactful discipleship with your students? What is your plan to get beyond the edge of the water?

NOTES

Introduction

1. Oxford Dictionary Online, https://www.lexico.com/en/ definition/post-truth.Accessed August 2019.

2. I borrowed this phrase from cartoonist Martin Shovel, http:// www.creativityworks.net/.

3. John S. Dickerson. *Hope of Nations: Standing Strong in a Post-Truth, Post-Christian World,* (Grand Rapids: Zondervan, 2018), 206.

Chapter 2

1. Darrell L. Bock. *Baker Exegetical Commentary of the New Testament:* Luke 9:51–24:53 (Grand Rapids, Baker Academic, 1996), 983.

Chapter 3

1. Time magazine article https://time.com/3858309/attention-spans-goldfish/. Accessed July 2019.

2. Research from Association for Psychological Science, http:// people.psych.cornell.edu/~jec7/pubs/cuttingetalpsychsci10.pdf. Accessed July 2019.

3. Jean M. Twenge, iGen: *Why Today's Super-Connected Kids Are Growing Up Less Rebellious, More Tolerant, Less Happy— and Completely Unprepared for Adulthood* (New York: Atria Books, 2017), 51.

4. Ibid, 50.

5. Barna Group, Gen Z: *The Culture, Beliefs, and Motivations Shaping the Next Generation* (Barna Group and Impact 360, 2018), 83.

6. James K.A. Smith, *You Are What You Love: The Spiritual Power of Habit* (Grand Rapids: Brazos, 2016), 144.

7. Ibid.

8. Frances E. Jensen, *The Teenage Brain: A Neuroscientist's Survival Guide to Raising Adolescents and Young Adults* (New York: HarperCollins, 2015), 66.

Chapter 4

1. Barna Group, Gen Z: *The Culture, Beliefs, and Motivations Shaping the Next Generation* (Barna Group and Impact 360, 2018).

2. Kara Powell, Jake Mulder and Brad Griffin, *Growing Young: 6 Essential Strategies to Help Young People Discover and Love Your Church* (Grand Rapids: Baker Books, 2016), 129.

3. John S. Dickerson, *Hope of Nations: Standing Strong in a Post-Truth, Post-Christian World* (Grand Rapids: Zondervan, 2018), 205.

4. Stephen Prothero, *American Jesus: How the Son of God Became a National Icon* (New York: Farrar, Straus, and Giroux, 2003), 8.

5. Ibid, 9.

6. David L. Turner, *Matthew: Baker Exegetical Commentary on the New Testament* (Grand Rapids: Baker Books, 208), 244.

7. James Emery White, *Meet Generation Z: Understanding and Reaching the New Post-Christian World* (Grand Rapids: Baker Books, 2017), 20.

8. John S. Dickerson, *Hope of Nations: Standing Strong in a Post-Truth, Post-Christian World* (Grand Rapids: Zondervan, 2018), 205.

9. Research cited from the Center for Bible Engagement, https://www.backtothebible.org/research. Accessed June 2019.

Chapter 5

1.   John S. Dickerson, *Hope of Nations: Standing Strong in a Post-Truth, Post-Christian World* (Grand Rapids: Zondervan, 2018).

2.   Barna Group, Gen Z: *The Culture, Beliefs, and Motivations Shaping the Next Generation* (Barna Group and Impact 360, 2018).

3.   David P. Setran and Chris A. Kiesling, *Spiritual Formation in Emerging Adulthood: A Practical Theology for College and Young Adult Ministry* (Grand Rapids: Baker Academic, 2013), 143.

4.   Christian Smith, *Souls in Transition: The Religious and Spiritual Lives of Emerging Adults* (Oxford: Oxford University Press, 2009), 46.

5.   Christopher Yuan, *Holy Sexuality and the Gospel: Sex, Desire, and Relationships Shaped by God's Grand Story* (New York: Multnomah, 2018), 10.

6.   N.T. Wright, *Paul for Everyone: Romans* (London: Westminster John Knox, 2004), 98.

7.   N.T. Wright, *The Resurrection and the Son of God* (Minneapolis: Fortress Press, 2003),250.

8.   David P. Setran and Chris A. Kiesling, *Spiritual Formation in Emerging Adulthood: A Practical Theology for College and Young Adult Ministry* (Grand Rapids: Baker Academic, 2013), 159.

9.   Ibid, 160.

Chapter 6

1.   Barna Group, *Reviving Evangelism: Current Realities That Demand a New Vision for Sharing Faith* (Barna Group, 2019).

Chapter 7

1.   Josh McDowell and Sean McDowell, *The Beauty of Intolerance: Setting a Generation Free to Know Truth and Love* (Uhrichsville: Shiloh Run Press, 2016), 43.

2.   Ibid, 96.

Chapter 8

1.   Jean M. Twenge, iGen: *Why Today's Super-Connected Kids Are Growing Up Less Rebellious, More Tolerant, Less Happy—and Completely Unprepared for Adulthood* (New York: Atria Books, 2017), 80.

2.   Greg Lukianoff and Jonathan Haidt, *The Coddling of the American Mind: How Good Intentions and Bad Ideas Are Setting Up a Generation for Failure* (New York: Penguin Books, 2019), 58.

3.   Ibid.

4.   Ibid.

Chapter 9

1.   Leah MarieAnne Klett, Hillsong writer: "I'm genuinely losing my faith." The Christian Post, August 12, 2019. https://www.christianpost.com/news/hillsong-writer-reveals-hes-no-longer-a-christian-im-genuinely-losing-my-faith.html. Accessed August 2019.

2.   Steven Kozak, *The Truth Is: Sharing the Truth of Jesus with Confidence, Conviction, and Compassion* (Chicago: Steven Kozak, 2018), 245.

3.   For further study on Erhman's views on Jesus, the Gospels, and early Christianity, see *How Jesus Became God: The Exaltation of a Jewish Precher from Galilee* (HarperOne, 2015)

or *Did Jesus Exist?" the Historical Argument for Jesus of Nazareth* (HarperOne, 2012)

Chapter 10

1. Harry Blamires, *The Christian Mind: How Christians Should Think* (Ann Arbor: Servant Books, 1978), 3.

2. David Kinnaman and Gabe Lyons, *UnChristian: What A Generation Really Thinks About Christianity And Why It Matters* (Grand Rapids: Baker, 2007), 123.

3. Barna Group, Gen Z: *The Culture, Beliefs, and Motivations Shaping the Next Generation* (Barna Group and Impact 360, 2018).

4. Alister McGrath, *The Passionate Intellect: Christian Faith and the Discipleship of the Mind* (Downers Grove: IVP, 2007), 21.

5. Nancy Pearcey, *Total Truth: Liberating Christianity From Its Cultural Captivity* (Wheaton: Crossway, 2008).

6. Andy Crouch, *Culture Making: Recovering Our Creative Calling* (Downers Grove: IVP, 2013), 64.

7. Alister McGrath, *The Passionate Intellect: Christian Faith and the Discipleship of the Mind* (Downers Grove: IVP, 2007), 20.

Chapter 11

1. Steven Kozak, *Certain: Erasing Doubts of the Christian Faith* (Rochester: Rochester Media, 2013), 35.

2. Andy Crouch, *Culture Making: Recovering Our Creative Calling* (Downers Grove: IVP, 2013), 92.

3. Ibid, 97.

4. Ibid.

PREVIOUS WORKS
BY STEVEN KOZAK

*The Truth Is: Sharing The Truth of Jesus
with Confidence, Conviction, and Compassion*
ISBN: 978-1982072810
2017, self-published

Certain: Erasing Doubts of the Christian Faith
ISBN: 978-1482378726
2013, Rochester Media

Printed in the United States
By Bookmasters